FIRESIDE READINGS.
VOLUME I.

"But seek ye first the kingdom of God, and His righteousness, and all these things shall be added unto you." Matthew 6:33

Lamplighter Publishing.
Waverly, Pennsylvania.

Fireside Readings.
Copyright © 2002 by Mark Hamby
All rights reserved.
First Printing, October, 2002
Second Printing, April, 2004

Published by Lamplighter Publishing; a division of Cornerstone Family Ministries, Inc.

No part of this edited publication may be reproduced, stored in a retrieval system, or transmitted in any form or by any means—electronic, mechanical, photocopy, recording, or otherwise—without prior permission of the copyright owner.

The Lamplighter Rare Collector's Series is a collection of Christian family literature from the 17th, 18th, 19th, & 20th centuries. Each edition is printed in an attractive hard-bound collector's format. For more information, write: Lamplighter Publishing, P.O. Box 777, Waverly, PA 18471, call 1-888-246-7735, or visit us online at www.lamplighterpublishing.com.

Various Authors
Printed by Jostens in the United States of America
Cialux #1593, M836 gold

ISBN 1-58474-042-6

PREFACE.

We are happy to introduce the first volume of our new collection of *Fireside Readings,* a compilation of short stories written long ago that will give your family hours of enjoyment together. Each story has been carefully selected to challenge, inspire, and give a message of hope in a day of uncertainty. May these new treasures be a blessing to you!

Mark Hamby

ROBERT'S TRUST.

BY

EDITH A. GIBBS

"HIS BROTHERS WERE ABLE TO ENJOY MANY AN HOUR OF AIR AND SUNSHINE."

A YOUTHFUL GUARDIAN.

CHAPTER I.

You will take care of the children, Robert, and see they do not get into any mischief! I can trust you, I know! I am sorry to be obliged to keep you at home, as it is so rarely you get a holiday, but I *must* take these dresses home myself, and see them fitted on. I promised them today, and if I were to disappoint, I should lose my custom."

"Right you are, mother dear! Don't be out longer than you can help. I'm due at the warehouse again at seven o'clock, and I should like to get a bit of a ramble after tea before going back to work!" replied Robert, in cheery tones, as he helped his mother on with her shawl. Then taking his baby brother up in his arms, he stood at the top of the steep flight of stairs to watch her receding figure, as, encumbered by a large parcel, Mrs. Archer slowly wound her way down, stopping for a moment when she reached the last flight, to kiss her hand to the baby, and to take a last look at Robert's bonnie, smiling face, before she started on her journey.

And Robert's was a face worth looking at, not so much because of any special regularity of features as for the frank, open expression of countenance, the pleasant blue eyes, and the kindly, cheerful smile; whilst the generally favourable impression of courage, health, and good temper was confirmed by a glance at the boy's sturdy, well-knit frame.

Nor was this a case in which "appearances are deceitful," for although Robert could run a race, or fight a battle as well as, or better than, most boys of his age, he was gentle with the weak, and by no means thought it derogatory to his dignity to lighten his mother's labours by taking charge of his younger brothers and little sister, or even by acting the part of "nursemaid" to the baby.

Fortunately for himself and others, the boy had been early trained in habits of self-reliance and helpfulness, which had stood him in good stead during the last year of poverty and trial; for not always had his home been in the midst of the noise and bustle of the city of Chicago, nor had the healthful bronze, which still lingered on his cheeks, been gained in the close confinement of the dingy narrow street, where we find him at the opening of our story.

No! when quite a tiny lad — before his parents left England — Robert's training had begun. And later — when, finding no outlet for his energies in the old country, his father had emigrated to the United States — the boy had learned to ride, and swim, and shoot; had followed his father for many a mile on foot, through the tangle of the great American forest, in the midst of which, far removed from other habitations, they lived a peaceful, healthful, and happy, if somewhat solitary life. Rising in the morning with the sun, free as the birds and busy as the bees, since depending as they did on their own efforts for their daily comforts, there was, for each one in the little household, some appointed task, which made the hours pass swiftly and pleasantly away, and the day seem all too short!

The only shadows on the brightness of these golden years were caused by the enforced absence at stated periods of Robert's father, whose occupation obliged him occasionally to leave his little household whilst he journeyed through the forest to some distant town.

Then, indeed, the hours would seem to lag, and to Mrs. Archer at least, the solitude of the vast wilderness would make itself felt, but less and less as years went by. She found in her eldest boy, young though he was, a companion and protector, none the less reliable; yet she knew how Robert was always longing for the time to come when Hal, who was more than three years younger than himself, might be able to take his place at home and set him free to accompany his father on his journeys, and share the perils and excitement of the way. For that there were many risks for a solitary traveler in that desolate region Robert well knew—better, perhaps, even than his mother, who had become so accustomed to seeing her husband return safe and well from his periodical expeditions as to have lost the dread with which she had at first always regarded his departure.

The more strange, therefore, was the undefined presentiment of evil which seemed to hang over her spirits the last time when, in answer to his usual summons, Mr. Archer had ridden forth, leaving her and the children to Robert's special charge. Even the father was not altogether free from the infectious sadness which oppressed his wife, and therefore more earnest then was his custom in impressing upon the boy the importance of the trust reposed in him, the necessity for courage, watchfulness, self-reliance, and patience which such a trust might involve — qualities which had been tried to the full, as week after week passed by and yet no news of the wanderer reached the weary waiters in the little cottage. Stricken down by an illness brought on by the anxiety and despair consequent on the terrible realization of her fears, the mother lay for weeks, incapable of thought or action, finding her only consolation in the mute and innocent caresses of the little child whose head just now was pillowed on Rob's shoulder.

That her husband had met with some terrible accident — had fallen into the hands of the Indians, perhaps had been murdered in the lonely forest — she could not doubt, though for a long time she tried to imitate her boy's unfailing courage, and to hope against hope. But the last thread which connected her with the happy past seemed broken when, following the advice of friends who had been raised up to help them in their distress, Mrs. Archer roused herself from her despair and removed with her children, and such of her belongings as she was able to retain, to the miserable lodgings up five steep flights of stairs in the midst of the great city, which henceforth must be their home, and where she was only too thankful to accept the chance of employment for herself and Robert, by which she might hope to keep starvation from the door.

There was one advantage — or, at least, so Robert tried to think — in being so high above the rest of the world, which was, that between the intervening crowd of chimney-pots, spires, and factory shafts, it was possible to get a peep of the not far distant hills, and to breathe a purer atmosphere than if they had been located on any of the lower flats. Then, too, they were undisturbed in their possession, since no one dwelt above them, and few cared to ascend the last steep flight of stairs; and — greatest boon of all — they had the sole, undoubted right of entrance to the leads, which, with a little contrivance, made a splendid playground. Robert had spent most of his leisure hours and all his small savings in the way of pocket-money, until with considerable ingenuity he had beautified the desolate region into the semblance of a garden. Here his little brothers were able to enjoy many a happy hour of air and sunshine without descending from their high estate, or coming under the demoralizing influence too often exercised by contact with the children who swarm in the streets and alleys of a great city. It was this last consideration which, more than anything else, reconciled Mrs. Archer to the daily toil of climbing the narrow staircase — this, and the fact that many a weary journey was spared her by Robert's thoughtful kindness, when his strong young limbs did duty for her trembling, weary steps.

That to have Robert at home for a whole afternoon to themselves was regarded as a great treat, an opportunity not to be neglected, was testified by the joy the children displayed as, having waved an adieu to his mother, he re-entered the little room, with little Effie clinging to his coat, and baby firmly perched upon his shoulder.

"Now, Rob, I vote we get to work at once on the garden. If you'll just come and tell us what to do, we'll run up to the arbour in no time," said merry, bright-eyed Hal, bustling about in a very important manner, and possessing himself of an old spade, a water-can, and a rusty rake. These were unearthed from the depths of a dark cupboard beneath the rickety little staircase leading out on to the leads, and, together with a small barrow of home manufacture, represented their whole stock-in-trade in the way of implements.

"Steady, Hal; there's no such great hurry; we've got all the afternoon before us. 'Business first, and pleasure afterwards' is my motto. It's too windy for little Trottie out there to-day, and it's time for his nap. I must get him off to sleep before I can attend to you. You and George can go out, if you like, to do some watering, and get everything in readiness, and Effie can sit quietly here and show Tom some pictures, whilst I walk up and down with Trottie. The quieter you all keep, the sooner I shall be able to get away. He's very drowsy already. Aren't you, old chap?" said Robert, kindly, as he settled the little fellow comfortably in his arms, and commenced pacing up and down the little room, softly humming a lullaby. The boys, obedient to his signals, crept out of the room, and little six-year-old Effie inveigled fidgety Tom into a corner, and kept him quiet and amused with a picture-book and a running whispered commentary of remarks, as cleverly as many a matron of sixty.

It was a very hot afternoon, and Robert was somewhat tired after a very busy morning at the warehouse, and a hurried run home through the crowded, noisy streets. Now, as he marched up and down, singing in sleepy tones, he began to feel very drowsy, and as if he should not at all object to a nap himself, if it were not for his promise to the boys. It seemed very probable that they would have to wait, for Trottie was in his most provoking mood, and declined to be shut out from his share of Robert in such a summary fashion.

"Me no' lie down. Rob sing! Me likes 'a song," he would say, lifting his thick lashes to take a roguish peep at Robert, just as the latter thought his efforts were successful, and prepared to put the little fellow in his cot.

"It's no use, Effie; I must take him into the

bedroom and rock him to sleep," said Robert at last in despair, as, at the sound of Tom's voice, raised in rather querulous tones, Trottie sat bolt upright, and stared about him, quite wide awake in a minute or two, and ready for any fun.

"Now, young sir! No more nonsense, please; if you don't go off soon I shall leave you to your own devices, so there!" said Robert, in decided tones, as, having shut the door, he ensconced himself in the rocking-chair, and closing his eyes to set a good example, swung slowly backwards and forwards, crooning his monotonous tune, until at last, not only did sleep visit Trottie's eyelids, but Robert himself went off into the land of dreams! The poor bare little room vanished as if by magic, and in its place he saw his happy woodland home; went back to that bright summer morning when, full of joy and gladness, he had ridden forth with his father to speed him on his way; saw once more the shadows chase the brightness from his father's face, as, with some dim foreboding of evil days to come, he gave the boy instructions how to act in case his return were delayed, and turning to take a last look in the direction of his home, bade Robert "do his duty, look after those at home, and trust in God;" then, after a final hand-clasp, he rode forth into the dark depths of the forest, and disappeared from view, whilst Robert, after vainly straining his eyes, and waiting for the chance of another farewell look, turned his pony homewards, feeling in an unusually sober and downcast mood, but resolved, come what might, to prove himself worthy of the confidence reposed in him.

Suddenly, however, the scene had changed. He was wandering, gun in hand, through a thick and tangled brushwood, beneath a scorching August sun. Every moment the heat seemed to grow more and more intense, until at last he felt he could no longer drag his weary limbs along, whilst the feeling of suffocation and oppression became so terrible he could scarcely breathe. Then came a strong smell of burning, and a curious crackling sound, which seemed to indicate a large fire close at hand. Already he fancied he could feel the hot blast blowing upon him, and see tongues of flame darting through the brushwood, creeping nearer and nearer to the spot where he had thrown himself down, utterly unable to move, though conscious how much depended on his promptitude in running home to warn them of the danger, for he knew of old how dangerously near the tangle grew to their dwelling. It maddened him to think he should be lying there inactive, helpless, powerless, when he ought to be using all the means in his power to avert the danger — that his boasted strength and courage had failed him in the moment of emergency! Ah, if anything should happen to those dear ones entrusted to his charge! How should he ever be able to meet his father's eyes, and acknowledge he had been "faithless to his trust"?

With this thought a new strength seemed to enter the boy; the spell which held him was broken; he started up, and was swiftly transported from the terrors of dreamland to a reality still more terrible, as by degrees he became aware of the fact that the sound of crackling and smell of burning were no dream, that the room was full of smoke, and Harold, with a very white, scared face, was peering in at the doorway, and calling to him to come and see what was the matter!

FIRE!
CHAPTER II.

For a few minutes poor Robert felt quite bewildered. He was still little more than half awake, and could scarcely disconnect the dream from the reality, but the sight of little Effie's terror and distress, as she rushed in and clung to him for protection, aroused him from his stupor. That the house was on fire he could not now doubt, so the sooner they could all get out of it the better.

Seizing a blanket from the bed, he wrapped it round little Trottie; then, taking Effie by the hand, and calling to Hal to follow with the boys, he made for the top of the stairs.

Alas! It was too late for hope of escape in that direction. The smoke was now rolling upwards in such clouds that, before they reached the lower landing, they were so choked and blinded that it was as much as Robert could do to beat a hasty retreat, dragging poor Effie after him.

"Quick, boys, up to the roof!" he gasped, groping his way up the narrow stairs, with Trottie, who seemed to have become stupefied with the smoke, still sleeping in his arms.

Once out in the fresh air, Robert felt his courage reviving.

"Hold baby a minute, dear. Be a brave little woman and help brother; the fire won't hurt you here!" said the boy, simulating a confidence he was far from feeling. He popped the little fellow on Effie's lap, and then, having closed the trap-door, ran to join his brothers, who were hanging over the little railing which bounded their garden in the front, and gazing down with an excitement, not unmixed with delight, at the noisy, seething crowd already assembled in the street below, which was becoming denser and denser every minute as the news of the fire spread.

"Oh, Rob, just see! They've got two engines, and here comes another! My, it's rare fun; I can see the flames down there, and clouds of smoke, and I do believe they're going to spout some water on the house!"

cried Georgie, making room for his brother beside him, and craning his neck over the railing that he might get a better view; whilst even Harold, although he would have preferred to be down in the street, and was looking rather pale from the alarm the first cry of "Fire!" had given him, was taken with the general excitement, and for a few moments forgot the peril of their position whilst watching the exciting spectacle.

Robert alone of all the children fully understood the terrible nature of the scene, or realised the awful danger to which they were exposed, cut off as they were from all communication with the world below; and it was with a feeling of helplessness amounting almost to despair that he looked vainly round for any means of escape.

On either side their little square of ground was walled in by a roof of shiny, slippery slate, sloping upwards to the chimneys.

To climb this roof, clamber across the narrow slab connecting the two stacks of chimneys, slide down the corresponding incline, and thus gain an entrance to the adjoining house, was a feat which Robert had once accomplished, when the mood for climbing was upon him; but it was a feat requiring, he well knew, no small degree of courage and coolness.

To attempt to get the children across would therefore be madness, whilst the thought of saving himself and leaving them to their fate never entered the boy's mind, or if it did, was banished as unworthy to be entertained for a moment. No, they were caught like rats in a trap, but at least they would all share the same fate; and there was still just a hope in the possibility of a rescue. If only they could attract the attention of the firemen, could make their position known, surely some attempt would be made to save them by means of the scaling-ladders which were about to be brought into service.

Quick as thought Robert sprang up, and vaulted the narrow railing; then creeping as near as he dared to the edge of the roof, commenced waving his handkerchief and gesticulating wildly. Fortunately for his project, the set of the wind was blowing the smoke away from the spot where he stood, and in the glare cast by the flames below, his figure was distinctly visible to those beneath, as was testified by a sudden roar from the crowd, then a silence, whilst many hands were pointed in the direction where not only Robert, but also the heads and shoulders of Hal and George could be seen, as following their brother's example, they waved their hats and shouted lustily. It was one thing, however, for those below to become aware of the existence of the children, another to render them any assistance; and the first wild tumult of joy which Robert had experienced at the thought of coming aid, gave place to a corresponding feeling of despair, as, gazing down from his giddy height, he watched the firemen, already engaged in their work of mercy in rescuing the poor sufferers from the lower flats of the burning house, and noted how inadequate were the means they possessed for reaching to its upper stories.

Suddenly a thought struck him! In the cupboard under the stairs was a long coil of rope, which he had purchased a few days previously, with a view to using it in the construction of his arbour. There was no saying how useful the rope might prove in an emergency, and anything would be better than to stand thus inactive; so creeping quietly back through the railings, and instructing the boys to keep to their post and continue the signals, Robert made his way towards the stairs, smiling reassuringly as he passed at Effie, who, seated on the little rustic bench, with Tom by her side and the baby on her lap, had recovered from her fright, and was fully occupied with her charge.

As he pulled back the trap-door the smell of burning and rush of hot air almost overpowered him, but with a short prayer for help, the boy determined to persevere in his purpose.

To dash down the steps, open the cupboard door, and seize the rope, was the work of a moment. But in that moment Robert realised their danger more fully than before, for in spite of the constant stream of water pumped on the house from the engines, the fire had made rapid progress; and it was tolerably evident that unless something should stop its course, their position on the roof would not be safe much longer.

Horror-stricken at the thought of their helplessness, and half suffocated by the smoke, the boy staggered up the steps with his coil,

"ROBERT FOUND HIMSELF IN A STRONG EMBRACE."

and shutting the door as quickly as possible, leant against the coping[1] for support, whilst he tried to collect his scattered senses. Hal's voice recalled him to the necessity for action.

"Rob, Rob, come quick! There's a man just below shouting to us, but I can't hear what he says. He can't get to us, I know, and the flames are worse than ever!" cried the little fellow, now evidently awake to the peril of their position, as he rushed towards Robert and dragged him across to the railing, pointing excitedly to where the figure of a man might be seen clinging on to the balustrade some thirty feet below, shouting and gesticulating to the boys to know if there was any possible way in which he could get to their assistance.

For all answer, Robert held up his coil of rope; then with hands that trembled as he thought of all that would depend on the security of his fastening, proceeded to knot it round an iron support which happily projected on the off side of the brickwork of one of the chimneys.

Here his early forest training stood him in good stead, and with the action came the remembrance of his father, and the lessons he

---

[1] the top or cover of a wall, made sloping to carry off the water

had instilled into the boy's mind of the necessity for promptitude and coolness in times of danger and difficulty. Bracing himself for an effort, he tightened the rope securely; then, carrying the rope to the iron railings, he threw the end deftly to the man waiting so patiently below. He peered over and held his breath for a moment in his anxiety to see if it would reach the required distance.

He was not left long in doubt. Almost before he knew what had happened, their rescuer had climbed up the rope like a cat, and Robert suddenly found himself clasped in a strong embrace.

"Father! You're here? Is it possible?" cried the boy, almost beside himself for joy and wonder as in the tall bearded stranger, whose eyes rested for a moment so proudly and lovingly on his face, he recognised his long-lost father.

There was no time for further words of inaction, for at that moment there came a piteous cry from little Effie, who stood just behind, now thoroughly terrified — "Oh, Rob dear, Rob, quick! Quick! The fire is coming after us!"

A HERO.
CHAPTER III.

What happened next, Robert could never very clearly recall.

He had a dim recollection of clouds of smoke and flame surrounding them in all directions; of helping his father to carry the frightened children to the front of the house; of watching Mr. Archer whilst he made the perilous descent with little Effie first, then the baby, then Tom, whom he handed one by one to the brave firemen who waited below to receive the children, and pass them down still lower; of vaguely wondering whether his father's strength would hold out for another journey; of looking round for little George, whose turn it would be next, suddenly to find him missing from the number.

With a cry of despair at the thought that he had forgotten his brother in his excitement, and had therefore been faithless to his trust, he had dashed into the smoke, to find the little fellow crouching in a far corner of the roof, apparently quite stupefied, and resisting all his brother's efforts to drag him into a less suffocating atmosphere.

After that, Robert knew nothing more until he awoke to consciousness, to find himself lying on a bed, his mother bending anxiously over him, her eyes full of tears. On trying to put up his hand to pull her dear face down to his to kiss, he found, to his dismay, that he had no power to move it, whilst a series of sharp pains in his body warned him that a broken arm was not his only injury.

Then by degrees, looking round at the long row of small white beds ranged on either side, and becoming conscious of the fact that he was lying in the ward of a hospital, he shuddered and groaned aloud. What had happened? Why was he lying in this strange place, and where were the children? Then he remembered what had occurred — the fire, the visit of his father, their rescue, and his horror on finding little George was missing.

"Where are they, mother? — the children?

and Georgie? I did try to save them, but he wouldn't come!" he said, in faint tones, his breath coming quickly in his anxiety to learn their fate.

"They are all safe, darling! Georgie, too; he was very badly burnt, but he is going on well; please God, he will recover!" replied Mrs. Archer softly, the tears coursing down her pale cheeks, as she bent lovingly over her boy. "Yes, and Father, too! It was no dream, my darling; he has come back to us once more, alive and well, as you always said he would!" she continued, in answer to the anxious pleading of the boy's eyes; which asked the question his lips scarcely dared to formulate. "There is much to tell, but I must not talk more now, or I shall not be allowed to stay by you. See, nurse is looking very reproachful already!" concluded Mrs. Archer, putting her finger on her lips to enforce silence, as she resumed her seat by the bedside; and Robert, well content to know by the happy smile which lighted up her worn face at the mention of his father's name that the sunshine had returned to her life, closed his eyes in obedience to her behest[1],

---

[1] command

and fell before long into a deep, refreshing slumber.

There was indeed "much to tell," as Mrs. Archer had said, but it was long before Robert was strong enough to bear the recital of all the marvelous adventures his father had gone through, neither have we time nor space to enter into details.

Suffice it to say that Mr. Archer had been overtaken by a terrible storm, when on his homeward journey, in the midst of the forest, had lost his way, and finally fallen into the hands of a party of Indians, who had carried him away captive into the interior, where, prostrate with fever, he had lingered for many months, hovering between life and death. How at length he had effected his escape, reached his home, only to find it desolate, and at last succeeded in tracking his wife and family, to find himself in danger of losing them forever, we must leave to the imagination of our readers.

That his efforts to avert this final catastrophe were crowned with a success beyond that he had dared to hope, was due, as Mr. Archer always declared, chiefly to the courage, forethought, and forgetfulness of self which Robert had displayed under circumstances when the absence of these qualities might well have been excused; and this opinion was shared by all who heard the story of the little English boy's "faithfulness to duty," which had made him stand to his post in the face of a terrible death, and risk life itself rather than desert those committed to his charge.

With that humility which is one of the most distinctive attributes of true courage, Robert was the last to imagine that there had been anything heroic in his conduct, and was therefore proportionately surprised and overwhelmed, when, one day — the first day he was allowed to be up and dressed for a short time — his father entered the ward bearing in his hand a letter and a small parcel, which he presented to Robert with a proud and happy smile.

"Father, what is this? There must be some mistake! These cannot be for me!" said the boy, his face flushing crimson, and his hands trembling with excitement, as, having gazed blankly a moment at the thirty-dollar note, which, together with a few lines, were the contents of his envelope, he hastily undid the parcel, to find a tiny leather case, and in the case a shining silver medal.

"No, Robert, there is no mistake! See, here is your name. If you read the inscription you will know better how great is the honour conferred on you, since this medal is awarded only for special deeds of courage and heroism, and never more deservedly than in the present instance, though it is I who say it! I am proud to think that I can claim a hero as my son!" said Mr. Archer, in a voice which betrayed his emotion, as, seeing the boy was too deeply moved for speech, he took the medal from its case, and pinned it to his son's coat.

It was a proud moment for Robert, as the children and nurses crowded round to see his well-earned and honourable decoration, but of more value in his eyes, than either medal or money, were his father's words of praise and his mother's happy tears.

FINIS.

"Therefore be ye also ready; for in such an hour as ye think not, the Son of man cometh. Who, then, is a faithful and wise servant, whom his Lord hath made ruler over his household, to give them food in due season? Blessed is that servant, whom his Lord, when he cometh, shall find so doing. Verily I say unto you that he shall make him ruler over all his goods."
Matthew 24: 44–47

"His Lord said unto him, Well done, thou good and faithful servant; thou hast been faithful over a few things, I will make thee ruler over many things. Enter thou into the joy of thy Lord."
Matthew 25:21

"He that is faithful in that which is least is faithful also in much; and he that is unjust in the least is unjust also in much."
Luke 16:10

Wilfred's Deliverance.

BY E. HODGES.

"Well, I don't believe in so much of that praying business. It seems a poor, mean way of getting out of scrapes. I believe in a fellow helping himself," and the speaker, a strongly-built, keen-eyed lad of fourteen, threw back his head with a defiant toss.

His companions, some half-dozen boys and girls, who, with a number of others, had just come from one of the children's services which were being held in the old city of Chester, were for a moment too startled by his words to answer them. Then a little girl of ten, with soft brown eyes and serious face, whose arm was thrown protectively round a younger lad, said, gently—

"*I* think it is nice to ask God for everything. But what should you do, Wilfred, if ever you got into a scrape that you *couldn't* get out of yourself, like Peter?"

Peter's deliverance from prison had been

the subject of the morning's lesson.

"It will be soon enough to think of what I'll do when the time comes," he said, jauntily. "At present I've never been in a bigger fix than I could get out of by the help of a little commonsense and determination. So never fear for me, Saint Hilda," and with a half laughing, half kindly look into the shocked little face, he turned down one of the straight narrow streets and was soon out of sight, while the others hurried away to their several homes, for it was already past dinner-time.

Mr. Bartle, the father of Hilda and little Dick, kept a second-hand bookshop. His wife had died when Dick was born, and since then his whole affection had been given to his children, whom, perhaps, he was rather given to spoiling.

From being so much with their father, Hilda and Dick had grown comically like him in tastes and habits. They would sit for hours, cuddled up in a corner of the shop, poring over some quaint old book, or weaving out of their own busy brains strange stories and wonderful adventures, which they would repeat, with merry laughing or well-feigned terror, to their father when the shop was closed.

No wonder Hilda's face grew pale, or that little Dick's eyes had a far-away look. No wonder, either, that such injurious habits angered sensible Mrs. Milchip, the housekeeper, or that every now and then she soundly rated her easy-going master.

Chester, as many of you know, is a very, very ancient city, possessing two things which no other English town can boast. These are its "walls"—which extend quite round the city, and upon the top of which is a broad pavement where people can walk—and its "Rows."

The Rows are really wide wooden galleries between the first and third stories of the houses, reached by little flights of steps. It is just as if the fronts of all the second-floor rooms had been taken out, leaving only the boarded floors, and big beams to support the weight of the house above. On one side are the shops, and on the other you can look over carved balustrades into the narrow streets below. The rooms on the floor underneath are let for warehouses, wine vaults, etc.

It was in one of these old Rows that Hilda and Dick lived, the ground floor of the house belonging to Wilfred Denning's father, who was a wine and spirit merchant.

Strange though this old city is above ground, it is stranger still beneath; for there have been discovered long passages, remains of temples and baths, and beautiful old crypts (small chapels), built by Roman, Saxon, and Norman hands. One of the most perfect of these crypts had been discovered under the very house where Mr. Bartle lived, and, I am sorry to say, was used by Mr. Denning for storing huge casks of wine and spirits. So that the place where men used to worship God was now occupied by that which too often makes them forget and deny Him.

At the far end of the crypt there was a vaulted passage, leading, it was supposed, to other underground chambers; but this had been boarded up some little distance within. Near to it, in a corner, stood the "bottling bench," where Evan Gyffen, better known as "Gyf," the old Welsh porter, spent most of his spare time. I have been thus particular in describing the crypt, because it was a

WILFRED'S DELIVERANCE.   41

favourite play-place of the little Bartles and of Wilfred Denning, the boy who "didn't believe in praying."

Wilfred's home was in another part of the city, and, after separating from his companions, he mounted one of the flights of steps leading to the walls, and hurried on. But the jauntiness had died out of his face, and it was cloudy and serious. He could not forget Hilda's words, though he had tried hard, whistling and even singing vigorously.

"Bother!" he exclaimed at length, impatiently; "I want my dinner — that's it. I'll take the short cut," and, stepping upon the low parapet, he sprang from the wall, which here on the inner side was only a few feet high, intending to strike into a path a yard or two away. But no sooner did his feet touch the ground than it gave way beneath him, and he felt himself sinking down, down! With a startled cry, he tried to scramble back, but the ground, loosened by recent heavy rain, crumbled at his touch. There was a swift rush, a crash, and he found himself in perfect darkness, lying upon something hard and level, his legs partly buried beneath loose earth and stones. For some minutes he lay too dazed to think or act, then, as his mind grew clearer, he exclaimed —

"I must have fallen into some old drain. If I can only get this rubbish off my legs I'll soon find a way out."

But the moment he began to remove the stones others rolled down upon them, and a sharp, stinging pain in one of his ankles made him fear it must have been badly injured.

"Oh, if I had only a light," he groaned, "just to see how to move! I shall be crushed to death!" and then, with a throb of joy, he remembered a few wax matches which had lain for weeks in a corner of his pocket. He struck one, and held it up. As the tiny flame shone out, he uttered a cry of astonishment, for it showed him no rough, narrow drain as he had supposed, but a place like a large, low hall, with pillars and heaps of rubbish, which must have dropped from above. He had evidently fallen into one of the old temples or baths.

For a few moments he sat still in the darkness and utter silence, considering what was to be done. Clearly, the first thing was to free his imprisoned limbs, and he lighted another

WILFRED'S DELIVERANCE.

match to see how this might best be effected; then he set cautiously to work, and by degrees got both legs free without seriously displacing the fallen stones. These he found firmly wedged in the hole, making it quite impossible for him to escape by that means, and for a moment his courage and confidence almost deserted him. But he soon recovered, and lighting another match, looked eagerly round in search of some entrance or passage.

To his great joy he saw something like one not far from where he had fallen; but the light died out before he could make sure, and fearing to strike another match—they were so few—he set out to feel his way, limping painfully on his wounded foot, and with frequent stumbles over fallen stones. At length he reached a wide opening which another match showed to be a passage, evidently leading somewhere; and with renewed hope Wilfred entered, feeling his way as before.

Soon, however, he was topped by a heap of rubbish, which seemed to fill up the whole space; but another precious match showing him a hole towards the top, he dragged his poor wounded leg up, and crawled through and down on the other side. Then, oppressed by the dense darkness and silence, he took out the last match and struck it.

Only just in time! A few more steps and he would have fallen headlong into a deep hole which stretched nearly across the passage.

With a shrill cry he started back, then while the light still lasted, crawled past it, looking fearfully for what might be beyond. There was nothing but the dense darkness; and as the friendly spark went out, he sank on the ground, partly from fatigue, partly from a sudden, terrible fear that perhaps, after all, he might not be able to find his way out.

"I could do it if it weren't for this wretched ankle!" he said, doggedly. "But how's a fellow to walk when he feels as if a dozen knives were sticking into him? I'll take off my boot and tie my handkerchief round."

He did, and for a minute or two it brought relief; then the pain came worse than ever, and he sank again upon the floor, the tears of pain and weakness—for he was faint from want of food—rolling down his cheeks. What was he to do? How escape? He was as

WILFRED'S DELIVERANCE. 45

fast shut up in this dismal place as Peter was in his "inner prison." And with the thought of Peter, came other thoughts: thoughts of his own sinful pride and self-will; of his wicked, daring words—for which he could not help thinking he was being justly punished. Of what use now were his boasted "commonsense" and "determination"? He should lie there and starve to death, and nobody would know. Oh, if he had anyone to pray for his deliverance as Peter's friends prayed for him! (Poor lad! like Hilda and Dick, he had no mother, and his father was too busy to think much about him.) Hilda would pray for him if she knew, he was sure of that; but then she did not know.

Choking back the big sobs in his throat, he tried again to think what to do. In vain: his mind, usually so bright, was dark and blank as the awful silence around him; and then in his despair he cried out, with an earnestness as intense as it was real—

"Oh, God, help me! I can't do anything, but Thou canst. Oh, forgive my wickedness, and deliver me from this dreadful place."

It was the first real prayer Wilfred had ever prayed. Would God in His love and pity hear and answer it?

*   *   *   *   *   *   *

"What is it, my maiden? Has anything vexed you that you're so quiet?" and Mr. Bartle put his arm round his little daughter as she nestled against his shoulder, and drew her forward tenderly. "Why, bless me!" catching sight of her face, "there are tears. What is it, dear?"

"I know, father," volunteered Dick, his large dark eyes moistening in sympathy; "It's Wilfred. He says he doesn't b'lieve in sayin' prayers. It's 'mean,' he says, and he can get along without."

"And is that what has been troubling my little girl all the afternoon?" said Mr. Bartle, pressing the tear-stained face closer to his breast. "Poor Wilfred. He does not know how much he misses, does he? But if he will not pray for himself, we can pray for him, you know."

"Like Mary, and Rhoda, and all of them did for Peter!" cried Dick. "Yes, that's it, Hilda!"

"*I have*," said Hilda, softly. "I did as soon as I got home."

"Then you may be quite sure that God will

answer you, my dear," said her father, kissing her as he lifted her from his knee, for Mrs. Milchip was calling "Tea-time!" from the inner parlour.

She eyed them keenly as they took their seats, and her face showed evident signs of displeasure which soon found voice.

"Well, I don't know whether it's these meetin's you children 'ave been going to lately, or whether it's porin' over them dusty old books, but you look whiter and more wizen-faced than ever! If the rain keeps off, Mr. Bartle, sir, you'll be pleased to send 'em for a good run round the walls; there'll just be time before dark."

The colour flushed up in Dick's small face, and he telegraphed a distressed look across to Hilda.

"Never mind, Dickey," she replied in her quiet tones, "I don't think the rain will keep off; Gyf said it wouldn't."

"A deal old Gyf knows about weather, burrowin' underground all day like a mole!" said Mrs. Milchip, sharply, for she was jealous of the ancient bottler's influence over her charges, whom she really loved in spite of her frequent scoldings. "I think, Mr. Bartle, sir, the children, leastways Hilda, is gettin' too big to be playin' down in wine cellars. I never did think as that crypt was a nice place for 'em myself."

"The crypt, nurse? Nonsense," laughed Mr. Bartle, for he was vexed to see the cloud on his children's faces, yet did not want to openly oppose his old servant; "why, where could they be better than in an ancient church? And Gyf, at any rate, is right about the weather," pointing to the window, against which great drops of rain were already beginning to splash.

The children gave a cry of delight, and scrambled down from their chairs.

"Do, father, please," pleaded Dick, "let us go down to Gyf to play. It's somefin' '*special*.'"

"Well, well, go along this once, just for half-an-hour; but mind, I will see you are out of doors all day to-morrow."

Scarcely waiting to kiss their thanks, they ran off, through the shop, out into the Row, and down the little flight of steps to Mr. Denning's office. They opened the glass door at the back, and as they did so, a low, quavering sound was heard, rising and falling.

"That's Gyf singin' J'ovah," said Dick, as they made their way carefully between the slim stone pillars, and immense hogsheads which stood beside Gyf's bottling bench.

The old man was fond of singing over his work, chiefly sacred songs, one of his great favourites being the grand old Welsh hymn:—

"Guide me, O Thou great Jehovah!"

He had just reached the last verse when the children entered, and as his weak voice quavered out:—

"Strong De-liver-er, strong De-liver-er,
Be Thou-u still my strength and shi-e-ld,"

one might have fancied it the cry of some lonely captive.

Some such thought seemed to strike little Dick, who exclaimed, "Why, Gyf, you might be Peter singin' in prison for God to d'liver you!"

"So I might, Master Dick, so I might. A grand man wass that Petarr."

"It was Paul and Silas who sang in prison, Dickey," corrected Hilda's gentle voice; "Peter was asleep. Don't you remember?" and she glanced expressively towards the doorway which led to the boarded-up passage.

The look reminded Dickey of the real object of their present visit, which for the moment they had forgotten.

"Of course; how silly I am!" he exclaimed. "May we have this, Gyf?" And Dick held up the end of a rusty chain.

"Yes, sure." Then, with an amused twinkle in his eye, he asked, "What is th' actin' this time? Is she the pris'ner of Chi-lon (he meant 'Chillon'), or is she Joan of Arrc, or one o' the Rooman marrtyrs in the 'rena?"

"It isn't any of them," said Dick, tugging at the chain, for it was long and heavy, "it's more serious. It is—"

"Come along, Dickey," interrupted Hilda, evidently not anxious for Dick to explain why they wanted the chain, "father said only half-an-hour, you know," and picking up the other end of the chain, she dragged him off towards the passage.

"Them two's th' quarest little mortals I wass ever come across," muttered Gyf when

Dick and Hilda were out of hearing.

And he was right. Accustomed, in their father's shop, to read any curious and ancient book whose pictures attracted them, they had become quite familiar with the histories of the heroes, and martyrs, and saints of old, and it was their delight, when they had read any story particularly thrilling or wonderful, to steal down to the old crypt, and, in their childish way, to act it all over again.

The story of Peter's deliverance, read and explained with such telling power at the meeting that day, had so impressed them, that they had determined to "act" it in their favourite corner of the ancient crypt.

They little thought that, this time, their play was to turn into a reality almost as strange and wonderful as the story they had heard!

Dick, of course, was to take the part of Peter, and Hilda, of the angel sent to deliver him; the soldiers they would have to "make believe."

It was darker inside the passage than the children had expected; they could see nothing but the walls on either side.

"I needn't go *quite* up to the boards," said Dick, shrinking a little from the still greater darkness of the upper end. "I'll lie down here."

"You can, if you are afraid," said Hilda, "but it won't be like Peter; he was in the 'inner prison,' you know."

"I'm not afraid," replied Dick, stoutly, "and we'll do it right. But you can't see to 'bind' me," and he threw himself down, the chain rattling sharply against the stones.

Hilda stooped to pick it up, but quickly raised her head with a startled look.

What was that—that strange noise? It sounded like a cry. Where did it come from?

She stood still with straining eyes, and lips apart. Again she heard it, and this time Dick heard it too.

"What is it?" he shrieked, springing up; "Oh, Hilda!" and together they rushed out into the crypt and threw themselves into the arms of the astonished old bottler.

"Matter is? Whatevarr!" exclaimed Gyf.

"Oh, Gyf, there's some one in the passage!" gasped Hilda.

"Shut up, 'prisoned!" echoed Dick, his dark eyes big with fright. "He's knockin'. Listen!"

And sure enough the sound of feeble rapping echoed along the passage. For a moment Gyf felt inclined to run too, for what dreadful thing might not be within there? But second thoughts brought courage. Loosing their clinging arms, he rose stiffly, murmuring under his breath, "My strength and shield," and hobbling towards the archway, peered in. "Who's anybody there?" he called valiantly. "Speak, whatevarr!"

"Gyf!" came faintly out of the darkness, "Oh, Gyf!"

"It's Wilfred!" screamed Hilda, as Gyf, backing in his astonishment, almost fell over them. "Wilfred, Wilfred!" and she ran into the passage, beating frantically against the partition as if her puny efforts could force the stout boards from their place; while Dick, as Wilfred's voice again reached them, turned and rushed up the crypt to the office, where he burst in upon the astonished Mr. Denning, exclaiming, as he pointed back into the darkness, "Wilfred, Mr. Denning! Wilfred, shut up—in the—passage—get him—out!" the last word rising almost to a scream from breathlessness and excitement.

For a moment, Mr. Denning simply stared

at him, thinking he had lost his senses; then suddenly recollecting that in this hasty rush home to dinner he had seen nothing of Wilfred, and that his eldest daughter, who kept house, was wondering what could have become of him, he sprang up, and, with Dick's small figure flying on before, hurried through the dimly-lighted vault.

As they reached the archway, Gyf was crying in shrill, reassuring tones—

"We'll get you out, Master Wilfred! 'Strong De-liver-er'!"

In a few minutes, with the help of a hammer and chisel, the boards were broken away, and Wilfred, pale and grimy, and half-dazed by the light, limped out. But the joy of seeing them all again was too much for his present weakness, and as the children gave vent to their feelings in a shout of delight, he fell fainting in his father's arms.

Mr. Denning carried him into the office, where he soon recovered sufficiently to tell them what had happened, and how he had been aroused from the faintness or stupor which had come over him by the clash of the falling chain, and, recognizing Gyf's voice, discovered that he had wandered into the passage which led to the crypt. So that at the time when he had given up almost all hope of escape, and lain down, as he feared, to die, he was actually within a few yards of the partition, only that the darkness prevented him from knowing it!

The doctor, who was hastily summoned, at once ordered Wilfred home to bed, the injured ankle needing perfect rest. But before the carriage which was to take him arrived, he beckoned Hilda, who, with Dick, was quietly weeping in a corner, to his side, and drawing her face down to his, whispered, "I believe in prayer now, Hilda. It was God who delivered me."

A bright smile shone out amid Hilda's tears, and she whispered back, "I know it was, because I've been praying too."

FINIS.

Jack's Hymn.

BY ELIZABETH OLMIS

St. Innocent's Hospital for children has, besides its spacious wards, its airy rooms, and its countless appliances for the comfort of its inmates, also pleasant nooks where the convalescents love to gather. In one of these, on a certain spring afternoon, several boys were sitting. The sunshine poured in through the great west window, tingeing with a brighter green the leaves of the tall plants which nearly screened the little group from observation. It filled the whole place with a kind of glory. The lads had been there but a short time when the sound of a crutch and of a halting step was heard approaching. Soon a golden head appeared around the corner of the leafy wall, and a slight figure came slowly toward them. The newcomer did not speak; he only smiled, and lay down on a low couch near Tom

Grey's wheeled chair.

The boys all smiled in return. They were fond of "Quiet Jack," in spite of his being so silent and strange. They went immediately on with the conversation which his entrance had, for the moment, interrupted.

"I tell yer it's the same one I've heered tell of afore," asserted Teddy Reilly, positively. "Once when I wor a leetle chap I got this 'ere same arm broke," he glanced down at his empty coat-sleeve, pinned across his breast, "an' I wor took to a 'orspetel, an' a young leddy comed ther' and fetched us flowers and red to us jes' like them dow that's bin here to-day. An' she telled us 'bout a man who could make us all wel ag'in 'thout no med'cin'. She wore a cross, too; not on her gown like these 'ere silv'ry ones is, but tied 'round her neck. 'Twor all yelled an' shinin' — gold, mebbe. She said as how this 'ere man could make even deaders alive ag'in, and — "

"That there's a good un, Ted," burst out old Bill Brady, with a scornful laugh. Bill was the largest of the boys. "How c'ud that be, I'd like ter hev yer tell? You're a silly to swaller all the stuffin' yer git, sonny."

Teddy flushed. Before he could answer, a soft voice from the corner made them all turn that way.

"It's all true, Billy," said little Donald Bliss. "I know, 'cause Mamma told me so."

The angry color died away from Teddy's face. Bill bent over and laid his rough, red hand on Donald's head. No one but the child knew how gentle this touch could be. All who could moved nearer to the cot where Donald lay nestled among the pillows. They knew how tender had been the tie between his mother and himself. They all remembered how sweet and kind she had been to them when she came every day to see him. They had not forgotten the morning when they learned that she would never come again. Their warm hearts were full of a deep sympathy for the little fellow. He could not walk, and every day when he was free from pain and felt strong enough, they begged to be allowed to push his low couch out to the place where they loved to meet and talk.

"Could ye tell us jest how yer Momma said 't was, Donnie, lad?" asked Teddy, softly.

Donald's great blue eyes grew very earnest. He raised himself and leaned against Bill's shoulder. It was very still as they listened to the "sweet story of old" — the story of Jesus, narrated in clear, childish tones. To most of them it was unfamiliar, save as they had heard it in the hospital.

"I wish't He was here to-day," said Tom, with a sigh, when Donald had ended; "I'd ask Him to make my hip ease up."

"Do you think He could be better to us than Doctor John is?" asked the small boy, who had not spoken before.

Loyal Donald hesitated.

"Doctor John is as good as he can be to all of us," he said at last, "but Mamma said that He could make blind people see and dumb people talk and lame people walk, and make everybody good, too."

No one noticed how eagerly "Quiet Jack" was drinking all this in. They were so used to his seldom speaking that they almost forgot that he could hear. He leaned nearer to Donald. His brown eyes were fixed intently upon him.

"To-morrow will be Easter," Donald went on. "You know that wicked people killed Him, but He made Himself alive again on

Easter Day. And so everybody is glad then. All the churches are full of flowers, and there is the sweetest music. I used to go with Mamma."

There was a sudden break in his voice. Memories awakened by the words he had spoken came thronging too quickly into his lonely little heart. He lay back upon his pillow, sobbing. Again Bill's hand smoothed back the curls. Silently the boys looked down at their companion; they felt big lumps in their throats. Presently Donald clasped his thin fingers about Bill's large ones. He smiled through his tears.

"Don't mind me, boys," he said, "I couldn't help it for a minute. Bring the books now, and let's sing the Easter hymn Miss Lillie taught us to-day."

Teddy and Bill rushed off and soon came back with half a dozen books. The place was quickly found, and the young voices, led by Donald's clear treble, joined in the grand rejoicing—"Christ the Lord is risen today."

At the first sound of the singing, Jack started. He put both hands to his head, then clasped them over his crutch, and closing his eyes, lay motionless as a statue.

Over and over again the boys sang the sweet old carol, until the corridor rang with its music. One by one, others gathered near and joined in. Those farther away caught up the refrain, and faintly from a distance came the echoing melody. When they had finished, twilight shadows were falling around them. They bade Donald good night. Bill and Teddy pushed his light cot back to his room. Jack alone did not stir. He seemed to be sleeping. After a while he got up and slowly limped down the long corridor. He met white-capped nurses carrying trays and going on various errands. He greeted them with his usual polite and pleasant smile. He kept on until he came to Doctor John's "den," as it was called—a small room just off the office—a place to which very few people were admitted. Jack was one of these few, for he and Doctor John were great friends.

Jack's face lighted up with pleasure when he saw the doctor sitting in a big easy-chair before the open fire. He stepped quickly to his side.

"Ah, Jack, old fellow!" said Doctor John, affectionately. "Come for our evening chat, eh?"

JACK'S HYMN.

He lifted the child to his knee; and Jack nestled down into the strong, kind arms in a way which showed how much at home he was there. One of Doctor John's hands was held tightly between both of Jack's, the other passed to and fro over the golden head which rested against his shoulder. They often sat in this way, without speaking, during the whole of the doctor's "rest hour." This is what he called their "evening chat."

But to-night Jack had something to say.

"Doctor John, please tell me about Easter. The boys were talking, but I—I forgot so soon. I try so hard to remember, but it all seems to go away out of my head."

There was a quiver in his voice.

"Does your head ache to-night, Jack?" asked Doctor John, quietly; "Let me rub it—so."

"Yes, it aches some. It always does. But not so very hard now, except when I try to remember. Sometimes, Doctor John, it almost seems to me as if I could, and—then—I forget again."

Doctor John's heart beat quickly. Could it be possible that what he had been hoping for and so patiently awaiting for many months was near at hand? That the strangely afflicted brain of this dear child was about to burst the fetters which had bound it? He spoke to Jack in his usual cheery way.

"So you want to know about Easter? Fix yourself comfortably, and I'll tell you."

In simple, graphic words Doctor John then told the story which had fallen from Donald's lips. Jack listened with close attention. He did not stir until his friend had finished speaking. Then he sat erect.

"Thank you, Doctor John," said the boy then. "I am tired now."

"And no wonder, laddie. It is suppertime this minute. Come, I'll get it for you to-night and put you to bed, too."

This was a special treat of which Jack was very fond. He smiled happily, but was too weary to talk about it. Doctor John laid him down among the cushions on his own comfortable lounge. Then he rang for a nurse, and when she had gone for the supper he took from his cabinet the prettiest china-bowl in the world, and a little plate, also covered with tiny blue flowers. These he placed on a small round table close to his big chair. Soon nurse came with milk and crackers; and

JACK'S HYMN.

Jack, again on Doctor John's knee, was being fed by his friend's hand.

"That was good," he said, looking up into the kind face when the last spoonful had been eaten. "Now, please sing. Sing what Miss Lillie sang to-day."

He cuddled down again contentedly. He heard the low, rich tones of the doctor's voice as he softly sang the Easter hymn. At first the same eager look overspread his face as when he listened to the boys; but gradually the lids drooped over the dark, bright eyes; the soothing melody quieted him; he was fast asleep.

Doctor John carried him to his little bed, dressed the slender form and laid it gently down. He stood for a moment looking at the peaceful face. He stooped and kissed it before he went away to his office for a long evening of study.

Nearly a year before this, Doctor John had gone to the mountains of New Hampshire for a short vacation. It was his old home, and he thought that he could rest better there than anywhere else. One day, when calling on some friends, he had seen Jack and had learned of his story.

"You remember the terrible collision on the X. and K. railroad last spring?" one of his friends had asked. "George and I were on the train, and escaped almost miraculously. We helped care for the injured as best we could. I remember the one lady who was nearly crazed with grief over the death of her only son, a little fellow eight or nine years old. His features were disfigured beyond recognition and his clothes burned to shreds; but she found a peculiarly-shaped knife of which he was very fond tightly clasped in his hand, and by this she was able to identify him. She was badly hurt, too, and was taken to a hospital in H. on the first train which was sent for our relief. I shall never forget the pitiful way in which she kept her eyes fixed on the place where she had lost her son as they were carrying her into the car.

We found another little boy who was severely injured; and who bore suffering so bravely that he won our hearts. He was not burned, but had been hit by something which made him nearly helpless. A day or two passed and no one claimed him. I said to George, 'We cannot go on and leave him to be sent to a hospital. If his friends do not come within a week let us take him home with us. Just suppose it was our Hal!'

So we waited, and then brought him here. We left our address with the physician, and one day a gentleman came who thought Jack must be his nephew, supposed to have been coming East on that train; but he found him quite another boy. No one else has ever appeared, strange as it may seem, and we now look upon Jack as our own boy the most affectionate, thoughtful, and lovable little fellow in the world, in spite of his loss of memory; for he seemed to have absolutely no recollection of anything previous to the accident, with the exception of the single word 'Jack,' which we suppose to have been his name. He is entirely well, and is slowly regaining the use of his left limb, which was for a long time useless."

Doctor John saw a great deal of Jack during his stay, and when he was ready to return he broached the matter upon which he had set his heart the first day he saw the boy. Mrs. Bernard was reluctant to even consider his proposition for a moment, but by degrees she was led to see that such a course must ultimately result only in the child's best good. She finally consented that he might spend a year in the Children's Hospital under Doctor John's special care. At first there had been slight change in him; but slowly, with increasing bodily vigor, came stronger mental action, and the doctor had great hopes of a perfect restoration of brain activity.

Jack's Hymn.

CHAPTER II.

In the early afternoon of this same day on which the lads were talking in the sunny alcove, in a handsomely furnished room many miles from St. Innocent's Hospital two young girls were arranging a quantity of cut flowers. They were at the same time conversing in low tones. Now and then they glanced toward a lady lying, apparently asleep, on a lounge near them, as though fearful of disturbing her.

"She is resting nicely," said the younger of the girls. "Poor Mamma! Easter time is always so hard for her to bear now. You know that it was on Easter Monday two years ago that Jack was killed."

"I suppose it all comes back to her so freshly. Do you think she will come over to church? The decorations are lovely this year."

"Oh, if only she would! But it is of no use to ask her. Jack was one of the chorister boys there, and he used to sing like a little angel. Mamma was so proud of his voice, even when he was a baby, almost. All this year that we have been in Europe we couldn't get her to go into a cathedral, for she was so afraid she might hear the boys singing somewhere. Papa and I both wish that she would go out more, and could get interested in something or somebody; she would be so much happier. But she seems to just live in the past with Jack."

"It is too bad. There, this bunch is large enough, don't you think so? I never saw such exquisite roses."

"Yes; Papa always gets the nicest ones. We arrange them ourselves, and Mamma takes them to the cemetery. Sometimes we go, too; but she spends every morning at Jack's grave. At Easter we always have a great many more than at any other time."

"They must cost much money," said Mildred, looking around at the numerous baskets filled with rare and perfect blossoms.

"They do cost a great deal," replied Alice.

JACK'S HYMN. 71

"You would hardly believe if I told you. It seems to me almost wicked to do it, even for Jack, when there are so many poor little children in the world. Papa and I often talk of it, and wish Mamma would be willing to adopt a little boy, not in Jack's place, of course, for no one could ever be to any of us what he was, but to take care of and to love. I believe if Jack could come back and talk to Mamma, he would want her to do this, for he was as generous and tender-hearted as he could be. He never could bear to see any one unhappy. But I don't suppose such a thing could ever happen — as Mamma's thinking of doing this, I mean," said Alice, sadly. "Dear Mamma used to love all the children, but she is so changed now. Our home doesn't seem like home any more. Mamma is so still and sad! Sometimes I think her heart is really broken, and that she can't love any one — not even Papa and me."

Tears were dropping on the flowers she held, and her lips quivered so that she could not speak.

"I'm so sorry!" murmured Mildred.

"I know you are," replied Alice, wiping her eyes, and trying to say cheerfully, "I'm not often such a baby. I cannot be, for Papa's sake; and I do try to be a comfort to Mamma. But—there, don't let us talk about it any more. We have these nearly finished. Then we'll run over to Hill's for another bunch of violets. Mamma likes them best of all."

They were not fairly out of the house before Mrs. Hunter arose. She had not been asleep. She had heard every word spoken by the girls.

They had pierced through the thick gloom in which her stricken heart had enshrouded itself. They strengthened a resolution which she had often made, but had always found herself powerless to carry out—a resolution to emerge from the seclusion of her grief, and arouse herself to her duties toward the dear ones still left to her. She loved them truly. She mourned over their shadowed home. She appreciated fully their exceeding tenderness and indulgence. But whenever she attempted, even in thought, to live again the active life which now seemed to have ended ages before, she shrank from it with inexpressible dread. How could she work and laugh and chat, and that without the dear presence of her beloved boy?

JACK'S HYMN.

But lately she had dreamed of him, and he had always seemed troubled. Once he had pulled at her heavy mourning veil, shaking his head as if in disapproval. Was he really unhappy over her selfishness (for she knew in her heart that she was selfish), or was it the disquieting influence of an uneasy conscience which haunted her sleeping hours? These and many other questions had been pressing upon her with insistent force which she had tried to ignore, but Alice's words and tears had aroused her effectually at last.

She called her carriage; in a few minutes she left the house, and the next two or three hours were busy ones. Having resolved to lay aside her somber garments, she determined that this day should be the last to see them worn. She was a woman who did nothing by halves, and she knew that a resolute will can accomplish much in a short time. At one of the large city establishments she found a suitable dress and wrap of soft, delicate gray. They needed but little alteration, which she patiently waited to have done. A bonnet — gray, too — with a lovely bunch of delicate blush-roses, half hidden among the lace, and long gray gloves, were soon purchased.

"These will do nicely for to-morrow," she thought, "but to-night? My courage fails me now as I look down at this black dress."

When, at last, she went home, the seat opposite her was piled high with packages.

Alice, meanwhile, had returned, and was much surprised to find that her mother had gone out.

"In the carriage, and alone, Celia? I can hardly believe you."

Celia smiled. She, too, had been surprised at the unwonted animation of her mistress.

"Yes, Miss Alice. And she told me to tell you to please go down to Hill's and get her some red roses. He has some particularly fine ones."

It was quite dusk when she returned. As she ran up the steps she noticed that the house was more brilliantly lighted than usual; but she was wholly unprepared to be met at the parlor door by her mother. She looked incredulously at the pretty arrangement of her hair, so long combed plainly back; at the gown of soft, white wool, with its creamy laces. She stood absolutely

JACK'S HYMN. 75

speechless as Mrs. Hunter took the roses from her hand and fastened a part of them on her breast.

"You wear the rest, dear," she said to the wondering girl. "And hurry, for Papa will soon be here."

Alice turned and went up the stairs without saying a word. She dressed with trembling haste, scarcely knowing what to think. This was certainly the sweet and lovely Mamma that she and Jack had been so proud of, but what had brought her back?

When she came down, fresh and charming in her simple dress, with the roses for her only adornment, her mother met her again. She kissed her lovingly; and arm in arm they walked up and down the long, fragrant room, which had taken on its long-lost homelike air.

"I did not thank you for taking that long walk for me, dear. To tell you the truth, I wanted to surprise you, as I could not unless you were far away. You have been so good and watchful of me that you don't let me stay long out of your sight. But I am going to take care of you now, Alice. I think you have lived without a mother long enough."

"Oh, Mamma!" was all Alice could say. She felt overcome with joy and wonder.

"Some other time, my dear, good child, we will talk together about it. Now we must keep our faces bright for Papa. Here he comes!"

Still holding Alice by the hand, Mrs. Hunter moved forward to the hall and faced her husband as he entered the door. As the girl had done, he looked about the room an instant in surprise; but his gaze soon centered upon the figures before him.

"We are glad you have come home, Jack," Mrs. Hunter said. It was the first time she had called him by his old, familiar name since little Jack had left them.

"Thank You, Jesus! Thank You, Jesus!" he exclaimed, tears flooding his eyes as he drew them both into his arms.

Jack's Hymn.

CHAPTER III.

Jack awoke very early in the morning after his supper in Doctor John's den, and the music of the Easter hymn seemed still ringing in his ears. Soon after breakfast he went to the office. No one was there but Cassius, busily engaged in "shinin' up" a whole case of already glittering instruments.

"Where is Doctor John?" asked Jack, eagerly.

"Up in de ward, Mars' Jack," replied Cassius.

"When will he come back?"

"Dunno, little Mars'. Not fo' chutch time, I reckon. He am pow'ful busy dis mawnin."

Jack looked so disappointed that kind-hearted Cassius inquired, as he carefully wiped off a keen-edged lancet,

"Wot yo' want, honey? Mebbe ole Cass' kin do it fur yo'."

The pale little face lighted up again.

"Oh, Cassius, please, please take me to the church, where—oh, you know what is there to-day, don't you? The—the—oh, I forget—But I do want to go, please, Cassius—just this once."

The great brown eyes looked up imploringly. The small fingers clasped themselves around the big black hand, while the child waited breathlessly for a reply.

"Tek car', dar, honey; dis knife's sharper'n lighnin'. Yo' cut yo'se'f, shore." The dangerous blade was carefully laid beyond reach. "Tek yo' to de chutch, honey? De bit chutch ober yander? Um—um."

Cassius, the faithful, devoted friend as well as the servant of Doctor John, knew something of the love which he felt for Jack and of the care which was taken of him, although, of course, he was ignorant of his malady. He now regarded the child keenly, and ready, with the true instinct of a sympathetic nature, the longing which swelled the little heart.

"Yo' jes' set down a minute, honey, outen de kurryder, 'twell I goes up an' ahsks Doctor John ef he kin spar' me fum all this ob wuk; den we'll be 'bout it," he said, at length.

He threw a light cloth over the table, carefully closed and locked the office door behind him, and trudged sedately away up the broad stairway, leaving Jack curled up on the low window seat, patiently awaiting his return.

It seemed to him a long time before he spied the shining, black face beaming upon him from a distance. He made his crutch fairly fly, as he hurried to learn the result of the interview.

"It's all right, little Mars'. De doctor say dat we kin go, an' he'll kum, too, jes' as soon as eber he kin."

"Oh, thank you, Cassius, thank you ever so much," cried Jack, overjoyed.

"And we will hear the music, won't we? And see the flowers; I remember that the boys—"

"Now, honey, de doctor say speshul," interrupted the old negro, "dat yo' mustn' talk none; dat I wuz to put yo' on de sofy 'twell I got de wuk don'."

"Oh, not in the 'den' all alone, please, Cassius. Let me stay out here with you. I won't touch a thing."

JACK'S HYMN.

Cassius laughed softly, showing every one of his white teeth. His eyes twinkled.

"Jes' yo' wait a minit, honey. Old Cass know how to fix yo'."

He brought some pillows and a thick, soft blanket, and made a nest across one end of the great office table. There he lifted Jack and laid him in it.

"How yo' like dat, little Mars'? T'ink yo' kin fin' de lan' o' Nod dat way?"

"It is as nice as can be. Now please hurry fast, Cassius, with the things. I'm going to watch you."

He did for a short time; but presently Cassius, glancing at him, saw that the lids were closing over the eager eyes. The queer-shaped instruments were deftly handled, and it was not long before the last one had disappeared within its own particular case. Noiselessly Cassius put them all away; then he stood looking down at the quiet sleeper.

"I suttenly does hate to wake dis baby up, he sleepin' so sweet, jes' like his own mammy watchin' ober him stidder ole black Cass. But I don' promise him."

Very gently he took one of Jack's hands in his broad palm.

JACK'S HYMN.

"Honey, open yo' eyes, now," he said, softly, bending down quite near, "Open yo' eyes an' wek up. Don' yo' hear ole Cass' callin' yo'? Don' yo' hear de bells a-ringin'?"

Jack stirred uneasily. He felt a touch on his shoulder. Turning, he saw Cassius standing beside him. At the same instant the church bells pealed forth their summons.

"Come," cried the child, starting up — "Come, it is time for us to go."

They walked slowly out through the hospital grounds and along the shady, quiet street which led to the church. They entered at a side-door and climbed a narrow stairway to a small side-gallery where Cassius was accustomed to sit.

Jack looked eagerly everywhere — at the beautiful stained-glass windows; at the memorial tablets; at the masses of exquisite flowers which filled the air with their perfume; at the people coming silently in.

Suddenly he heard the sound of faint, sweet music in the distance; nearer it came, clearer, stronger; the mellow tones of the organ joined softly in. Far down the dusky aisles he saw approaching the white-robed choirboys; the harmony swelled to richer fullness; in loud, triumphant strains, jubilant and joyful, they sang the glorious tidings—

"Christ the Lord is risen to-day."

Keenly, intently, Jack listened. With his whole soul in his eyes, he leaned forward, clasping his hands. Not a movement of the singer nor of the rector escaped him. The service went on. By and by he laid his head against Cassius's shoulder and closed his eyes.

Cassius, careful not to disturb him, made all the responses, and listened with devout attention to the reading of the lessons.

Again the tones of the organ, rich and deep, were heard. The boys stood up and began a hymn. Jack sprang from his seat; the restless, troubled look was gone from his face—a beautiful light shone on it. Leaning on his crutch, pale, fearless, he joined in the singing.

From above suddenly floated down to the wondering congregation the silvery, bird-like notes of a marvelous voice, pure and strong. Of almost unearthly sweetness, with a strange, thrilling accent of rejoicing, it filled the place. Looking upward, all eyes were fixed upon the radiant child. The hymn was ended; softly the organist played on. Again Jack sang his Easter hymn, amid the breathless hush of the multitude.

At its close he saw Doctor John standing by his side. He sprang into the out-stretched arms, crying, joyously,

"Oh, Doctor John, I can remember now — I can remember now! Where is Mamma?"

When they were again sitting quietly in the "den," Jack told the doctor of his pleasant home in the distant city — of his sister, his papa, and his mamma; of the journey East on which he had started with her; of his going to another part of the car and talking with a little boy there.

"He was traveling alone to Boston, Doctor John. He said he had no home, and was going to live with his uncle. I had just shown him my knife that Papa brought me from Russia, when all of a sudden I felt the car tipping over. Something hit me on the head, and I didn't know anything more about it until today."

Doctor John waited with intense impatience for a reply to the telegram he sent to Mr. John S. Hunter, No. 38 Winship Street,

Toledo. Was there really such a man, or was all that Jack had told him but the vagary of a diseased imagination? The time seemed endless until he read upon the yellow blank before him the words:

We leave at once. Expect us on 7 A.M. train, Monday.
JOHN S. HUNTER.

Seldom in his life had the young physician felt more deeply moved. Without doubt, this mother who was coming was the very one of whom Mrs. Bernard had said, 'She was nearly crazed with grief over the death of her only son.' He realized that it was no slight thing for him to have a part in the restoration, as if from the dead, of a son like Jack.

The boy was, apparently, none the worse for this sudden return of his memory. Even the doctor's observing eye could detect no sign of the reaction he had feared.

"Are you sure they'll be here in the morning, Doctor John?" he asked, when he kissed him good night.

"Not sure, laddie, but almost so. Go to

sleep now, quickly, so that Mamma will find a bright Jack waiting for her."

"I'll try, dear Doctor John," putting his arm around his friend's neck and hugging him close. "I love you next to Mamma, Papa, and Alice."

Jack's Hymn.

CHAPTER IV.

The next afternoon the boys had gathered as usual in the pleasant corner. They were telling Donald the wonderful news about Jack, when they heard his voice nearby. Immediately he came around the plants as he had done before, only now he held by the hand a happy-faced, smiling lady. The boys arose.

"This is my dear mamma, boys," Jack said. "Mamma, this one is Teddy, this is Bill, and this one in the wheeled chair is Tom Grey. They have all been good to me; and this is dear little Donald that we love best."

Mrs. Hunter shook hands with each one and said some pleasant word. But she stooped and kissed Donald's cheek and held his hand in hers as she talked with them. Jack leaned against her knee, too happy to do anything but look at her and listen.

A few days later he bade them all good-by, for he was going home; and who but blue-eyed Donald was going too, to live there always as his own loved brother.

"Don't ye forget us, Donnie, lad," said Teddy. "When me an' Bill gits well and earns a bit we'll come out ther' an' see ye."

"Oh, yes," began Jack, with his face aglow; but stopped suddenly. "I forgot that it was going to be a secret," he went on; "but never mind. Something nice is going to happen to you boys next summer. Dr. John knows; don't you, Doctor?"

Doctor John smiled mysteriously.

Jack did not explain any further. He went about the rooms and corridors, speaking a pleasant farewell word to everybody, his face beaming as he promised to come back soon to see them again.

Teddy and Bill stood looking after the carriage as it rolled out of sight.

"Thet 'ere's a big thing fur Donnie now, eh?" said Bill.

"That it is, Bill," replied Teddy. "'T aint ev'ry leetle chap as gits such a mother when his own be's gone."

Then, after a long silence, during which

he seemed to be thinking perplexedly, Bill asked,

"Ted, who d'ye think made Jack well? Wor it Doctor John?"

"No, Bill. I think 'twor the man wot Donnie telled about."

FINIS.

Eric's Good News.

BY AMY LEFEUVRE.

Such a sweet little face it was, with the curly golden-brown hair clustering round the fair white brow, and the deep-blue eyes with their gaze of wistful longing. The flush on the soft cheeks hinted of delicate health, and many a passer-by noted with pity this frail little figure leaning back in the cushioned chair.

But Eric did not heed them; his eyes were fixed on the ocean in front of him, and not even the joyous shouts of the children at play, as they built and demolished their sand castles and forts, seemed to attract him.

His nurse was engrossed in a book; she was accustomed to her little charge's silent moods and after settling his cushions and drawing him into the shade of the cliff, now composed herself a little farther off on some flat stones to enjoy an hour's quiet.

"I wonder if it's as tired as I am, poor thing!" came at last from the little lips.

A young man who was lazily reclining some few yards off now looked up sharply as he caught the words.

"I wish it would be tired enough to keep still," he said.

Eric turned his large blue eyes upon him.

"It tries to be still, but when we are very, very tired we can't be."

"We have not the strength left to resist the force that drives us; quite true, little chap."

The child was silent for a minute, and then added softly; "I saw it asleep yesterday; it was so still, just breathing a little and panting at the edge. It couldn't help doing that; no one can be quite, quite still."

The young man smiled, and the two drifted into a quiet, lazy conversation, strange to hear between two such widely opposite characters.

"It's a weary world, isn't it?" asserted the child, with an old-fashioned gravity. "Nurse is very fond of saying it is, and I think so too."

"One soon gets to the end of it," remarked

the man, with a bitter smile.

"It is all the same isn't it" – except surprises, and I think I've finished them."

"How long ago is that, little chap?"

"My last toy from Paris, I think. Father says he won't bring me any more, because I didn't feel it a surprise, and I don't care for things if they don't surprise me. I suppose I am too big for surprises now. Everything is always the same, isn't it?"

"Always, little philosopher, when you get accustomed to them."

"I wondered in one of my thoughts today if I shall ever see anything very, very wonderful. It seems so long when nothing happens."

"What would you like to see?"

"Ah, I don't know; I shouldn't like it unless it was a surprise – something that would make me – make me different. I should like to feel quite, quite comfortable, you know – I mean, in my heart. I suppose I mean happy. I should like that, wouldn't you?"

"There is none of that kind of happiness in this world, unfortunately."

"Nurse says there is, but she isn't happy. I think it is only in books and dreams, don't you?"

"It is a fancy, not a fact; but you are rather too small to talk so."

"I remember feeling happy once," and the child's eyes shone with a soft, glad light. "It was when I was a very little boy, and I went into the country to a farm; and I was very tired, and the woman there caught me up in her arms and carried me into a long room all red with the fire. It was such a funny room, with plates and dishes all up on the walls, and there were baked apples for supper, and pork, and a cat with a bell round its neck; and nurse said I must go to bed, but the woman said, 'No,' and she cuddled me up against her and said, 'Bless his darling little heart!' She was rather plump and very soft, you know, and I sat on her lap all the evening. She told me such beautiful stories; I have never heard them since, and father told me they weren't true; she said they were, but I know better now."

"'Puss in Boots' and 'Cinderella,' eh?"

"Oh no, no! Much more lovely – about a place up there!" and the small white fingers were raised to the blue sky above. "I forget it; a kind of paradise, all love and happiness, and something about a wonderful man who came down here from it. She said He loved me; but I've forgotten now, and father said it wasn't worth remembering – only made up to amuse babies!"

There was a curious smile on the young man's lips. His was a restless, dissatisfied face, a face on which the traces of a misspent life and of blighted hopes had already left their marks. Though comparatively young in years, he was old in the ways of the world; for he had lived fast; and because he had exhausted all the resources of the world's pleasures, and had been disappointed in love, he now had come to the conclusion that life was not worth living.

He glanced at the innocent young face beside him and then up into the unfathomable blue.

"Not worth remembering!" he muttered, "why, no – of a certainty not."

A silence fell on them; the boy's deep blue eyes were scanning his fresh acquaintance very closely.

"I like you," he said quaintly, at last, "because you talk to me as if you understood. Nurse says I'm discontented because I am spoiled and because I have everything I want. Father says it is because I am ill and not like other boys; they are so rough and noisy, and they never do anything but rush about. They won't sit still and talk to me, and if they do they say I am an 'odd fellow,' and then they leave me. Do you think I am odd?"

"You and I are in the same boat, old fellow! We are tired of life, are we not? And those who are still enjoying it cannot understand."

"I want to be happy," the boy said wistfully, as his eyes wandered over the blue ocean before him, "quite happy – right through, I mean. Do you think I ever shall be?"

The young man made no reply, and at this moment the nurse came toward her little charge.

"It is time to be going home, Master Eric," she said, glancing at his fresh acquaintance as she spoke.

The young man rose to his feet. "An only child?" he questioned, as he stood in the full strength and power of his manhood, looking down at the frail little invalid.

"Yes, sir; only son of Sir Edmund Wallace, who owns most of the property about here."

Her tone was dignified and she stooped down to arrange the cushions before she wheeled the little carriage away, adding as she did so, "His father has just gone abroad for a month or two, so he feels lonely, poor child."

But Eric shook his golden head.

"No, I'm not lonely, and I hear very often from Father. I like letters, but talking is best. Will you be here tomorrow, sir? I don't know what your name is."

"Captain Graham," the young man said with a laugh. "Yes, perhaps you will find me here tomorrow."

They bid farewell and the young captain strolled away.

"Sir Edmund Wallace, the great skeptic!" he muttered in the wind. "Ah, well, I more than half believe he has right on his side."

Eric's Good News.

CHAPTER II.

Another morning found this strange pair together. The young man, in spite of his cynical indifference to all around, found within himself a growing interest in the quaint, sweet speeches of Eric Wallace.

"There is no one in the world that can manage the sea, is there?" the little fellow said, as he lay watching the rough waves dashing against the breakwater and scattering themselves in showers of white foam upon all that came in their way.

"No one," his friend replied. "Don't you know the story of the king who placed his chair on the sands when the tide was coming in, and forbade the waves to come any farther?"

"What a silly man!"

"He wanted to teach his courtiers a lesson, for they thought him divine."

"What is divine?"

"Being able to do everything," he answered hesitatingly.

"I should like to be divine. Do you know what I should like to do?"

"No."

"I should like to be able to sail away up there to that white cloud, away from everybody and everything, and just lie down and wait till the sun sets, and then sail right into glory."

"What glory?"

"You have seen it – all the golden streaks, and pink and red – so lovely; there must be something behind it all. Do you read fairy tales?"

"I used to, I fancy."

"Father won't let me read many books; he says my brain can't stand it. I am rather tired of fairy tales. What kind of books do you like? Nurse reads novels; father reads science. Do you like reading?"

"I am busy reading the books of nature at present, and – you."

"Now that is nonsense; you can't read me!"

At that moment Eric's large retriever, who

ERIC'S GOOD NEWS.

always accompanied his little master to the beach, and who had been frolicking about in the sea, now appeared with some tattered leaves in his mouth, which he dutifully brought to the little invalid's couch and deposited.

"Good Rex!" said the child, as he took it from him. "Rex always brings me things from the sea, but he knows I don't like old shoes and rubbish; he used to bring me those, but I taught him not to. This is part of a storybook; look! I shall dry it and read it, only don't tell nurse. She won't let me read anything, now Father is away, unless she looks through it first. She says it is as much as her situation is worth!"

The boy was carefully smoothing the wet leaves, and Captain Graham took it from him saying, "It is most likely trash, my boy. I shouldn't keep it."

But having looked at it, he gave it back to him with a curious smile, saying, "That can do you no harm, at all events."

"Oh, thank you! I like to read when nurse leaves me to get her tea. You see, I get tired of talking to Rex; he is generally with me. Why don't dogs talk, Captain Graham? We do."

"We are a higher development of human nature," was the grave reply.

"I don't think dogs get as tired as we do, do they? And they always seem happy. I should not mind being a dog."

"Without a soul?"

Eric's blue eyes were opened wide.

"What is a soul? Cook says sometimes, 'Bless my soul!' and I asked her what it is, and she laughed and said, 'A fish.' But I didn't believe her, and I asked Father; and he said some people thought they had souls, but science proved – I forget now. What do you call a soul?"

"We are getting into deep water; supposing we change the subject. When is your father coming back?"

"Not for a long time. What is a soul, Captain Graham?"

"Upon my word, I don't know. It is supposed to be the quality in us that makes us superior to animals. Don't you feel yourself much more clever than Rex?"

"No; the only difference is that I can talk and read, and he can't; but then Cook's father can't read, and nurse told me she knew someone who couldn't speak. We aren't much alike in looks, are we?"

Captain Graham threw his head back and laughed aloud.

"Not much, my boy, certainly!"

"Do you know, I heard nurse's sister say once to her, when they were talking about me and whether I should live to grow up, 'Poor little fellow, and his father thinks he will die like a dog!' How does a dog die, Captain Graham?"

"He comes to an end – goes out like a candle; and people say we do not."

Eric's earnest gaze disconcerted the captain.

"Tell me what you mean. How do we die?"

"What does your father say?"

"He doesn't like me to talk about dying, but he said once it was going to sleep and never waking up. Is that what a dog does?"

"I suppose so."

Silence fell upon the pair; both were looking out on the ocean and both were thinking. At length a deep sigh came from Eric.

"Well, I'm tired enough, anyhow. The time goes so slowly, and everything is always the same; it never changes."

"Life is not attractive to either of us, eh, my boy?"

Eric smoothed out the pages of the book he held in his hand without replying.

"The – Gospel – according – to – St. Mark," he read out slowly; "What a funny name! What is gospel, Captain Graham?"

"It means 'good news,' I believe."

"Do you think this is a true story?"

"I believe so."

"Have you read it?"

"Yes, I used to read it when I was a little boy."

"Is it only a story for little boys?"

"A good many people read it. Look at the sea this morning; isn't it uproarious?"

Eric's blue eyes turned seaward.

"Don't you think it gets angry sometimes? It is quite in a passion this morning, and no one can manage it. I should like to see some one who could. It wants to get beyond the breakwater and it can't; that's one thing that is able to stop it. It is no good the waves making such a fuss and noise, is it? They never do any good by being so rough."

"I think they enjoy it. 'Come along,' say they; 'let us upset the boat. It is such fun to see the men floundering about before they sink forever! And then let us frighten the children and knock down those ridiculous sand forts they're building. If only we could get a little farther and sweep away every creature on the sands, what glorious fun it would be! Don't you think they would like to have us, Eric?"

"You make them out cruel. They will be sorry for their roughness soon, and then they'll try to go to sleep; that's when I like them best."

This proved to be the last conversation Eric held with his friend for some days, for Captain Graham went to London on business; and it was not till a week later that he again sauntered along the sand in search of the invalid carriage with its little occupant.

Eric's Good News.

CHAPTER III.

"Hullo, little chap! You are looking quite spry! What have the doctors been doing to you?"

Eric's weary wistfulness had indeed vanished, and there was eagerness and interest in his expressive little face.

He put his little finger to his lips in a quaint, old-fashioned way as he glanced at his nurse, then held out his hand to the captain. Looking up at his strong stalwart frame, he said very winsomely,

"Do you like me, Captain Graham?"

"Who does not, you young fisher?"

"But do tell me! Are you fond of me?"

Captain Graham laughed heartily as he gazed down at the boy.

"What is coming, Eric? Out with it! Do you know that I have strolled down on purpose to see you this morning? Being one of the most selfish and lazy of human creatures, that says a good deal for your attractive power, let me tell you!"

"I want you to lift me out of the carriage and carry me to that rock over there and let me sit on your knee, like Father does," Eric said softly. "Only tell nurse you are going to do it first, or she will be coming after us. I want to have a quite private talk with you."

It did not take long to carry out this desire, and as Captain Graham held the light little frame in his strong arms, he said,

"Why Eric, a puff of wind would blow you away!"

"I am not heavy, am I? Now then, you must listen, please, because my mind seems

so very full that I must talk. I have wanted to talk to you so much. You see, I haven't let nurse see it; she doesn't know I have it, and you and I understand things, don't we? You don't call me discontented and peevish, because you feel it yourself, don't you? You know what I mean – you are unhappy and tired like me, and we want things to be new instead of old."

"Just so. Old philosopher! Go ahead! I'm listening!"

Eric's eyes grew brighter, and the pink flush deepened on his cheeks, as he drew carefully out of his pocket a little brown paper parcel. Opening it slowly, he disclosed to Captain Graham's amazed gaze the few pages of the Testament he had taken home with him.

"You said it was true, Captain Graham," the child asserted with an emphatic nod, "and it is wonderful!"

"Is it, my boy? I am glad you found it so."

"But, Captain Graham, have you ever read it? Such a story, and such, oh, such a good man! I love Him! I cried when I was in bed last night because I didn't live when He did. Oh, if only I had! If I only could have just seen Him! And there is such a lot I don't understand, and such a lot I want to ask you about. Do you know, He could do anything. Fancy! He was going to cross the sea one day with some men, and He was so very tired, He just put His head down and went fast to sleep; and the waves got rougher and rougher, and the water came into the boat, and still He was so tired, He went on sleeping. The other men were so frightened that they woke Him up and told Him He didn't care for them, whether they were drowned or not; and then what do you think He did? He just stood up and looked, and saw the rough waves, and all the sea trying to tip the boat over, and he told it all to be still at once, and it was! Wouldn't you like to have been there? And that isn't all. He just walked on top of the waves another time, when the other men were all in a boat by themselves and there was a storm; He went to them like that!"

The boy's face was enthusiastic as he looked seaward, and stretching out his hand, he said, as if to the ocean, "No one can manage you now, but you have been made still once, and it was grand, grand! I should like to have seen you crushed under his feet! O Captain Graham, why did you never tell me about this wonderful man before? And Captain Graham, who is God?"

"My boy, you are going into matters too deep for me; better give me that book and forget all about it." The captain looked uneasy as he ran his fingers through the curly golden hair resting against his shoulder.

"But I must know! Forget it – as if I could! And it is all true; I feel it is true, and you said it was!"

"Did I? I don't think I did."

"Captain Graham, isn't it true?"

The startled look in the blue eyes, as they were raised in all-trustful innocence to his, stopped the denial already on the young man's lips. As yet, though the little faith he possessed had nearly been extinguished by his willful acceptance of the doubts that had assailed him, there was in the depths of his heart the remembrance of a mother's faith and teaching, and of days gone by when he too had listened to the same old stories that were now absorbing the interest of the child on his knee.

"It will be interesting to watch the influence of the teaching on him," he muttered, adding aloud, "Yes, it is true, Eric, to those who are able to accept it."

"Then who is God, Captain Graham? For this man was his son."

"God made the world," the young man said reluctantly. "He made everything you see, and is still – so people say – ruling over all, though invisible to mortal eye."

"And He is alive somewhere?" asked the child.

"He can never die."

"Where is He?"

"He is supposed to be everywhere."

"I don't understand. Where is heaven?" Up in the sky? Because it says Jesus was 'received up into heaven at the right hand of God' and I heard some one say once that it was a good thing there was a heaven up there. I asked Father what it meant, but he said heaven was another word for sky. O Captain Graham, I want to know such a lot of things – do be quick to tell me! And do you think Jesus is still alive? Now— today – is he? Because, do you know, it was so wonderful! I cried and I cried and I cried about it, but I never thought it possible for such a happy end to come; and after He was buried He came alive again, and I shouldn't like Him to die again. Is He alive today? Was this story written a very long time ago?"

"You should ask one question at a time, my boy. And what an excitable little mortal is he! Why, you are quivering from head to foot! Suppose we change the subject. Nothing in this world is worth such excitement."

"But this is about another world, and that's what I want to know. Is there another world? And how can we get to it? And is Jesus there? O Captain Graham, you might tell me if you know!"

The back of Eric's small hand was brushed hastily across his eyes, but it did not hide the tears already swelling up; and Captain Graham began to realize that the very depths of the child's soul had been stirred – that this was no light matter with him.

"Eric, I will tell you what has been told me, my boy. Now listen!"

Slowly and haltingly, but gathering strength from the intensity of longing and expectation from the blue eyes that gazed upward into his, Captain Graham told the child the old, old story. First he spoke a few words about the creation, then about sin entering the garden, and the plan of salvation, and the future life for each believing soul, Eric now and then stopping him with eager questions, which required clearer explanations.

The time soon slipped away, and Eric's nurse appeared on the scene.

"I am sure it is very kind of the gentleman to be troubled with you, Master Eric. It's rarely, sir, he takes to strangers so. He's such a child for keeping to himself!"

"Captain Graham, will you be here tomorrow?"

"Perhaps I may."

"My head is so full that I want to have one of my thinks now. But there's a lot more I want to understand."

"Take care that little head doesn't burst! I fancy the brains inside are too big for it now."

As Captain Graham watched the little carriage being wheeled away, he drew himself up with a stretch and laughed, "Wouldn't my old mother have been proud if she had heard me holding forth this morning! It may be worth my while to take up preaching as a vocation – anything for a change!"

Eric's Good News.

CHAPTER IV.

When Eric saw Captain Graham coming up the beach the next morning, his face was full of excitement.

"I have something I need you to do for me, Captain Graham," he bellowed, waving a fine parchment envelope in the air.

"For goodness' sake, Eric. You're going to fall out of your chair!"

"I can't help it, Captain Graham. I have a letter I want you to send for me right away. You may read it, first, in case I may not have written quite properly."

By now Captain Graham was sitting down beside Eric and took the envelope gently in his hand. Eric watched his friend with nervous scrutiny while the captain carefully pulled the letter from the envelope.

"Would you like me to read it out loud, Eric?"

"Yes, yes – that would be wonderful! Then

I will hear how it sounds."

Captain Graham unfolded the letter and began to carefully read the words:

"'Dear Jesus, I thought I would like to write to tell you that I love you. I wish I had known about you before, but I am so glad you are still alive. I wish I had been one of those children you took to your knee, because you were so kind. Would it be possible for me to come to heaven to visit you? I don't know where it is, but perhaps you can send for me. I would very much like to come. My friend Captain Graham says you died to save sinners. I don't know what a sinner is, but I will ask him more about it. I think it was very wicked to kill you, but my book says that they could not do it quite; and for that I am very glad. I hope you will answer this letter soon and tell me I can come and see you. I am your loving Eric Wallace.'"

"Will it do, Captain Graham?" Eric pressed anxiously. "You will send it to Him, won't you?"

"No, my boy, I cannot do that. What has become of your wise little head to think of such a thing? How is it to go?"

Eric's lips quivered. "I thought – I thought

ERIC'S GOOD NEWS.

the telegraph wires, or balloons, or something – I thought you would know. O Captain Graham, there must be a way to heaven! I so want Him to get my letter."

A quick sob was choked down, and the captain, who had the boy on his knees, drew the curly head to rest on his shoulder as he said soothingly,

"Don't cry, Eric; you need never write letters; if you say your prayers it will do just as well."

"What is prayers?" sobbed out poor Eric.

"Well, talk to Him as you do me. He hears everything. He is God, you know, and God is Spirit. He is close to us now, though we cannot see Him, and you have only to speak and He hears at once."

"You mean I can talk to Jesus whenever I like? Do you mean it, really?"

"Yes, I believe you can."

Eric was silent for a minute, and then his eyes fell on the letter now resting on his lap.

"And this is no good," he said sorrowfully. "I had better tear it up then."

Just then a gust of wind swept past them and seized the paper into its clutches, tossing it wildly in the air. Their eyes watched in wonder as it was carried away, waving triumphantly, up and up and up, and finally out of sight.

"Captain Graham! God has told the wind to blow it up to Him. He does want to see it!"

"It certainly looks like it."

"I'm so glad; it took me so long to write. And now, Captain Graham, what is a sinner?"

"Anybody who sins – does bad things – is wicked; anything wrong is sin."

"Nurse says telling lies and hiding things is wrong. I expect I'm a sinner; I have been hiding this story of Jesus from nurse. Is that wrong?"

"I expect so."

"Are you a sinner? I mean, have you ever been one when you were a little boy like me?"

"We are all sinners, Eric. The bigger the man, the bigger the sinner, I believe. Yes, I'm a pretty big sinner, I expect."

"I'm so glad," said Eric, cheerfully. "Then Jesus died for you and me. I don't quite know what that means; but it is something good, didn't you say? Tell me again why He

ERIC'S GOOD NEWS.

died."

"Upon my word, Eric, I can't explain it. Your book tells you."

"It's rather difficult to understand, Captain Graham, and you did tell me about it yesterday. Tell me again."

"Well, I believe if He had not died we couldn't have gone to heaven, and now we can."

"When can we?"

"When we die."

"But I have heard they put people in the ground. How can they go to heaven?"

"That is only their bodies. We are supposed to have souls that leave our bodies, and that part of us goes to heaven."

"It's beautiful!" exclaimed Eric, with shining eyes. "And now tell me what heaven is like."

"I don't know" – a gleam of humor shot into his eye. "I have never been there, you see."

"But you told me yesterday a lot about it."

"Oh, that was what the Bible tells us about it."

"The Bible? That is what my father told me wasn't fit for little boys. Go on – tell me about heaven."

It is a beautiful place, Eric, all goodness and happiness, and everybody and everything quite perfect. No worries, no bills or duns for money, no deceivers, nothing hollow or sham, no hypocrisies and pretenses, nothing to mar one's enjoyment."

"And Jesus is there!" broke in the child's voice softly. "That will be best of all. If He would take me up in His arms I should be quite, quite happy forever. Do you think He would?"

"I think He might."

"But why couldn't we have gone to heaven without Jesus dying? That's what I don't understand."

"Because God could not let a sinner enter heaven. He said we must be punished for sin, and that was separation from Him forever. But Jesus Christ said, as He was not a sinner, He would be punished instead of us; so He came down from heaven and lived a good life here, to show us how we ought to live. When He died it is supposed that He bore all our sins on Him then, and so God forgave us."

"And now you and I are going to heaven?"

ERIC'S GOOD NEWS.

"I don't know about that."

"But you said we were sinners. We are, aren't we?"

"A good many sinners will be shut out of heaven, Eric – so people say."

"Why?"

"I am a bad hand at this my boy. Don't you think we have had enough of it?"

"But," objected Eric, his lower lip drooping pitifully, "I don't want to be shut out of heaven, Captain Graham, and I don't understand you. You change round. You said Jesus died to let us go to heaven; why can't we go?"

"So you can, and you are pretty sure to get there, too!"

"Then you can go too, can't you?"

"If I wanted to, I suppose I could."

"But don't you want to?"

"I have not thought about it."

Eric looked puzzled, but he had faith in his captain, and felt sure, if his words at times were difficult to understand, it was because he was grown up and knew a great deal more than himself.

"My doctor is coming to see me tomorrow," Eric said after a long pause. "He comes from London every two or three months to see me; so I sha'n't be here tomorrow morning. He is very kind, but he does poke me about so, and always goes away saying, 'You must rouse yourself, my boy!' As if he hadn't roused me enough by all his pokes and shakings!"

"What does he think he can do for you?"

"He told Father once there was no reason why I shouldn't live to be a strong man. He said I wanted to be roused and amused, and then Father took me round the world in his yacht, but I was no better after, and I got tired of that before I got half round."

"You are hard to please, youngster."

"Not now I shouldn't be, Captain Graham. That tired feeling has nearly gone; only I wish I understood more about the things in my Good News."

A still longer interval now elapsed before Eric met his friend again. The weather proved stormy, and the beach was deserted by all save those who considered themselves impervious to wind and rain.

Captain Graham grew restless as he paced up and down in his comfortable quarters at the Royal Hotel.

"I have stayed here long enough. Thank goodness, my leave is nearly out! Any kind of work will be better than this; and yet how sick I am of our set of fellows! I have half a mind to sell out, but what on earth should I do with myself then? I cannot imagine what is keeping me here, unless it is that child. He ought to be put in a book. The correct thing is for him to die, I suppose, but he seems to have taken a new lease on life. I can fancy his father's wrath when he comes home and discovers what subject is engrossing his thoughts. Shall I be held up as his teacher, I wonder?"

And this thought was so ludicrous that Captain Graham indulged in a hearty laugh; yet there was a hollowness in his mirth, and a heavy sigh quickly followed.

Eric's Good News.

CHAPTER V.

The captain was seated at luncheon a few days later when an envelope was brought and handed to him. Upon opening it, he found a small note from Eric.

"My Dear Friend: I want you to come and see me. Nurse said you would not be troubled, but I know you will. I can't go out because it is raining so. I am very happy, and I have written to Father and told him all about it. Nurse has been very angry, but she says she's only angry because Father will be angry. I don't know what she means, and I want you to tell me. Come soon, please. Dr. Parker has told me a lot more.

Your dear friend,
Eric Wallace"

An hour after found the captain swinging along in his mackintosh toward Broughton

Manor, a large bag of hothouse grapes protruding from one pocket, and a packet of French bonbons in the other. He found Eric on a couch in a luxuriously furnished room overlooking the fine old park that surrounded the manor.

Eric's face lighted up as he held out his little hand to his visitor.

"I knew you would come. I have missed you so! I have such a lot to tell you. There is Father's easy-chair there; it's a very comfortable one, and I don't mind you sitting in it, though I never let anyone else, not even my doctor."

Captain Graham seated himself with a smile, and then brought out his gifts. Eric's face brightened even more.

"You are a kind friend," he said quaintly, as he held out both hands for the parcels and eagerly pulled out a bonbon.

"Do you know you are the first visitor I've had here all for myself? Would you like a bonbon too? I could ask the butler to get you some tea if you like."

"No, thank you," said Captain Graham with a twinkle in his eye. "You enjoy them all yourself. Now what have you been doing with yourself during this stormy weather? Been moped to death, eh?"

"Oh no, no! Why, Captain Graham," Eric said as he leaned forward impressively, his blue eyes glistening with emotion. "I have been learning to know Jesus. Would you like to hear?"

The young man leaned back in his chair and crossed his legs.

"Very much, Eric."

"Well, it was my doctor who helped me. When he came to poke me about, I said to him, 'Isn't it a pity, doctor, that Jesus isn't here to make me well without any poking? I wonder if you know about Him.' And then he said he did, and he sat down and told me just to speak to Him as if he was standing by my chair, because He was really there, only I couldn't see Him. And then he knelt down on the carpet, just here between you and me, and he spoke to Him himself, and then he asked me if I would like to speak to Him; so after a few minutes, I did. I felt rather shy, you know, at first."

"And what did you say, my boy?"

"I said, 'My dear Jesus, I hope you'll excuse me speaking to you, because I know you are a wonderful person, but my Good News tells me you're so kind to children that I know you'll listen to me. I want to thank you so much for dying for me, and I am glad to find out that I am a sinner, because you are fond of sinners. I don't know you very well yet, but I do love you. Will you please be my friend, and will you talk to me when I'm feeling uncomfortable and lonely?' I think that was all I said to Him. I reminded Him that I had sent Him a letter, and asked if He liked it. I think that was all."

"And what happened then?"

"Well, then the doctor told me a lot more. Fancy! I can ask the Lord Jesus for anything I want, and if it is good for me, He will give it to me! I suppose you know that, don't you, Captain Graham?"

"Yes, I suppose I do."

"But isn't it lovely? And I've asked Him such heaps and heaps of things. And He has answered some already. I asked Him to give Sarah's mother some washing. Sarah is one of the housemaids who is very good to me, and her mother is so badly off she can't get meat more than on Sundays. And He sent her a lady yesterday who gave her some;

ERIC'S GOOD NEWS.

Sarah told me this morning. And I've asked Him to find our black kitten and send her home, and not to let Father be angry, as nurse says he will be. And I asked Him to make you come and see me today; nurse said you would not be bothered. And then I told Him about Cook, who will send rice puddings for dinner and says they're good for little boys, when she knows I don't like them. I asked Jesus to make the rice bad, so that she couldn't cook it. And then I remembered Simmonds's nephew, who has broken his leg and has to leave off being a sailor. His young lady, Simmonds says, won't look at him, so I've asked Him to make her kinder. I can't tell you all. I talk and I talk to Him, and the best of all is that He is never tired of listening, my doctor says, and that He is always with me."

"And how did your doctor find you, Eric – better?"

"Yes, much better. He says I have found the medicine that would make me well at last. I don't know quite what he meant, do you?"

"I think he may have meant you had found something to interest you, my boy."

"Well, I don't feel tired inside now. This is the biggest surprise I have ever had. I wish someone had told me about it before. And then, Captain Graham, I find that I can do things that please Jesus. He likes me to be patient, and not tell nurse she is a crosspatch, and not throw my medicines away when they are nasty. He wants me to grow up as much like Him as I can be; and of course, you know, this gives me a lot to do, because I have to stop and think very often before I do things. I used to try to be good because nurse said I ought; but I know now it makes Him sorry and grieved, and I don't want to make Him sorry. I do love Him so!"

Captain Graham leaned back on his cushions with a bit of a sigh and gazed thoughtfully out the window. He was happy for the lad.

"It seems to me, Eric, that you have learned all you can learn, and more than most in this world. I have something else in my pocket for you. I am leaving in a week's time. I have to go back to my regiment, so I thought I would give you a complete copy of your Good News, as you call it. If your father doesn't like it he must take it from you when he gets back. You have got something in your head now that he will not be able to take very easily, and if it makes your life happier, it would be cruelty to deprive you of it. Tell your nurse that I gave it to you, and that as things are, she had best let you have it."

Captain Graham placed a New Testament in the little fellow's hand. It was a handsome copy bound in Russian leather; and when Eric knew what it was his smile grew perfectly radiant.

"You're very good to me; I don't know what I shall do when you are gone. I wish you wouldn't go. You see, you know all about these things, and we can talk about them together. I shall have nobody if you go. My doctor isn't coming down to see me for a long time. Would you be very angry if I asked the Lord Jesus to make you stay?"

"I think you had better not, Eric. Look! I do think the weather is breaking! There is the sun again. Won't you be glad to be down on the beach tomorrow if it is fine?"

"Yes," said Eric, contentedly, as he fingered his new treasure, "and I hope you will meet me there. Will you?"

"Yes likely; but I think I must be going now."

"Wait a moment. Will you ring that bell, please? I can't get up."

And then, a solemn old butler appeared.

"Simmonds, this is my friend, Captain Graham. You haven't seen him before. He is a very old friend now, and a very nice one. I like him better than the friends you and nurse try to find for me; but I chose him myself – at least, we did it together; didn't we, Captain Graham?"

"That we certainly did, Eric."

"And, Simmonds, Captain Graham has brought me the most beautiful Good News that you ever saw, with a lot more in it than mine has. And it's Captain Graham, you know, who has shown me how to be happy at last, so you ought to thank him. You were always saying you wished I wouldn't be so miserable. He told me all about Jesus first."

The old butler smiled kindly on the child.

"He does look wonderful better sir; excuse me."

And then noiselessly he slipped out of the room; and after a few minutes Captain Graham took leave. As he tramped back to the town his thoughts were busy.

"It is a wonderful thing for satisfying a child's soul," he said to himself. "I wonder if it will last, and if by any possibility – granted that I could believe in it – whether it would satisfy mine!"

Eric's Good News.

CHAPTER VI.

The weather broke, and there were very few mornings that did not find the young soldier on the beach by the side of his little friend. Sometimes Eric would ask to have a chapter read out of his Testament, and then would follow an earnest discussion. At least, if the earnestness was only on the child's side, Captain Graham did not let him see it, and the questions and deductions that sprang up struck the captain as startlingly fresh and conclusive. But the last morning came, and Eric's bright little face grew so very sad when the time of parting drew near.

"Will you write to me something, Captain Graham? I shall be thinking of you often."

"I promise to send you a line now and then, my boy."

"And, Captain Graham, I've been very puzzled lately; I can't make it out and I'm so sorry."

Eric paused, gazing wistfully up at the face

of his friend, and then shook his head very sorrowfully.

"What is up now?" inquired Captain Graham, in an amused tone.

Eric slipped his little hand into the strong one that was laid on his shoulder.

"I wonder why you are so unhappy if you have known all about Jesus. I should never have been if I had known before, and yet you were just as tired and unhappy as I was."

"It isn't so fresh to me as it is to you, Eric."

The captain's tone was hesitating; he could not bear that the boy's faith in him should be shaken, and yet truth compelled him to undeceive him.

"I had forgotten all about these things, my boy. They don't touch me as they do you. It is my own fault, I suppose. You know much more about them already than I ever did."

"Why," said Eric, with eyes wide open, "you have told me all yourself! And you have explained all the hard things so beautifully. Why, Captain Graham, if it hadn't been for you, I should never have known about Jesus."

"It isn't knowing about Him that makes you a Christian, Eric. It's letting that knowledge of what He has done for you touch you so deep in your soul that it changes you – gives you new life. Don't puzzle your little head over me. You are a happy little soul in your belief; keep so, and when you pray to your new Friend, don't forget me."

Eric nodded brightly. "He knows all about you, Captain Graham; I have told Him everything. I will ask Him to make you happier. He is sure to do it. Oh, must you go?"

The young soldier stooped down and let Eric's two little slinging arms grab him round his neck. His quivering lips pressed tightly against the captain's bronzed cheek.

"Good-bye," Eric said as he gathered his courage. "I'll try not to miss you. I don't mind disappointments so much now; but I sha'n't never, never forget you!"

Poor little Eric's ungrammatical sentence rang in the captain's ears as he walked away, 'I sha'n't never, never forget you;' and he grimly wondered what his brother officers would say if they knew in whose society the latter part of his leave had been spent.

"Ah, well," he muttered, "I envy the child's faith and happiness, and more than half feel inclined to follow his example. It is not a religion he has ahold of, but a real person; it makes a vast difference, I fancy."

Captain Graham rejoined his regiment, and his life went on in an old way. Yet he looked forward with a strange pleasure to the letters that arrived from Eric. And he vainly endeavored to stifle the uneasy, restless longings in his own heart. It was after receiving one of these quaint epistles, one evening, that the young man retired to his room with a fixed purpose in his mind – that of settling once for all whether there was anything in this religion for him, or whether it was only suitable for innocent children.

"I cannot stand the worry of it much longer," was his angry thought. "I cannot imagine why it has taken such a hold on me; do what I will, I can get no rest from it night or day!"

He spread the child's letter before him.

"My dear, dear friend: I was happy to get your nice letter, and I like hearing about the bugles and the soldiers and your clever horse. I'm getting well so fast that my doctor wrote and said perhaps I could try walking with crutches instead of being drawn in my carriage. I should like that. My dear father has been taken with a fever. He has never written to me since I wrote to him and told him what Good News I had found. He wrote to nurse and told her not to scold me, for I would forget it all very soon. I don't understand what he means. Do you? I am asking the Lord Jesus to make him better and send him back quickly. My dear captain, are you any more happy now? I get happier every day. I tell Jesus about you, and I feel He is sorry for you too. He likes people to be happy, my Good News says. Have you told Him what's the matter with you? I expect you have; but there is nothing He can't do, is there? The most wonderful thing He has done for me was finding my knife. I lost it, and it's got my name on it, and Father gave it to me, and I have lost it for months; and when I knew He would give me anything I wanted, I asked Him to find my knife. I told nurse I should get it, but she laughed; and yesterday Rex brought it to me in his mouth. He had found it in a heap of dry leaves in the garden. It was kind of Jesus to tell Rex where it was. He knows how fond he is of finding things. Rex was so pleased, and so was I. I must not write any more, nurse says.

Your loving friend, Eric."

"Have I told Him what is the matter with me? Of course I have not. I don't know myself. If this Book is true, I shall never be at rest till I have done so. And I do believe the truth of it in my soul; only how to set to work is the difficulty. Eric slipped into it easily enough. If one were a child again it would be easy enough, but as I am not – "

Captain Graham here started. He had a Bible in his hand and had been carelessly scanning its pages; but now here before him were these words, and they burned themselves into his very soul as he gazed:

"Except ye be converted, and become as little children, ye shall not enter into the kingdom of heaven. Whosoever therefore shall humble himself as this little child, the same is greatest in the kingdom of heaven."

Long did he ponder. When midnight came it found Captain Graham on his knees.

"Lord, I believe; help thou my unbelief."

Eric's Good News.

CHAPTER VII.

As the captain was finding his way to Jesus and a happier life, many miles away, Eric was waiting for Simmonds to read a telegram that had just arrived.

"Is it news from my father? Please read it to me quickly," Eric pleaded.

"No Master Eric, it is from your aunt in Plymouth." Simmonds answered quietly. "It says your father arrived in port just yesterday. He is gravely ill, but implores that he must be brought to Broughton Manor. He will not rest with the doctor's counsel to wait until he is stronger, so she has booked passage on the next train. They will arrive late tonight."

Eric's eyes moistened as he looked up at Simmonds.

"O Simmonds, he must make it home. I have so much to tell him."

Tears now began to fall from Eric's cheeks.

But suddenly there was a glimmer of light in his eyes. Eric hobbled to his father's study on sturdy wooden crutches. The months had brought with them a growing strength in his legs and he no longer depended on the old carriage. He sat down at his father's desk, pulled out a piece of paper and began to write in the best handwriting he could muster.

"My dear Captain Graham, I am in trouble, and I so want to cry. But I must be brave. I have been told that father is gravely ill. He is trying to get home. I am sure it is because he wants to see me and see for himself all that has happened to me. But he is so weak my aunt must bring him. She knows all about Jesus so I think He is watching over him. I cannot imagine that my dear father should die. Please come if you can. I know you will be able to tell me what to do. Your loving friend, Eric."

He quickly folded the letter, put it in an envelope and called Simmonds into the room.

"Simmonds, could you please address this and mail it right away?"

"Yes, Master Eric," he answered.

But he did not go to the post office. Instead, he made a straight path to the telegraph office and wired the news directly.

When he returned, he found Eric sitting in his father's old chair with head bowed in prayer. Finally, the comfort of sleep fell upon him, so deep that he did not hear the travelers arrive late that night. It was just as well, for the trip had taken its toll, and Eric's father was barely able to stand. He was quickly taken to his bed.

"I am not sure what is keeping the man alive," Eric's aunt said to Simmonds.

"Perhaps Miss Wallace, it is Master Eric's prayers."

"Yes, you are probably right. There seems to be some unfinished business between them. How is the dear boy?"

"It is like a miracle, that little one's faith. He has turned this house upside down with it – happiness, you know. He can even walk now in short paces."

"Well, if that does not win my brother's heart to Jesus, I do not know what will."

When Eric awoke the next morning he found Rex sitting alert and staring at him.

"What is it, Rex? You look ready to charge.

Has father arrived? Is he awake?"

Rex stood quickly, pacing in a way that Eric knew he must follow.

"I'm coming boy. Remember, I am not so fast as you!"

Eric followed Rex to the sitting room on the west side of the house and found that it had been made into a bedroom for his father.

"You stay here, Rex," he commanded as he stroked his back.

Eric entered the room ever so quietly, making his way to the chair by the bed. He did not see that his father was awake and watching him. He didn't see the tears that began to flow down his pale cheeks.

"Eric, is that you?" his father whispered, trying to reach out his hand.

"Yes, Father," Eric answered. "Be still, I am here. I knew Jesus would bring you home."

"Just look at you my boy – walking! I thought surely the doctor lied to me in effort to cheer me. You know I am dying, don't you? I have to come to see you. I had to know the truth. I am so proud of you. Look how strong you are."

"Oh Father, it was when I was weak that

ERIC'S GOOD NEWS.

Jesus found me. He came to help those who cannot help themselves."

"Eric, you are such a good boy. I can not tell you how often I have read your letter."

"Oh Father, I am so glad. I had wondered if you were angry at me." Why did you not send a reply?"

"I was angry, my son. That is why I could not write. But no longer, Eric. Please remove the letter from my pocket and read it to me. I will so enjoy hearing your words from your own mouth." So Eric read aloud the letter he had written to his father:

"My darling Father: I have a lot to tell you today, and you will be so glad to know I am happy at last. I have found the wonderfulest book, which means Good News, and it is all true. It came from the sea, and Rex brought it in his mouth, and Captain Graham told me a lot more. I wish I could tell you what's in it, but I can't write so much. There's a wonderful man, so good and kind, in it. I loved Him when I read about Him; and He really was alive once, only He was killed; but He came alive again, because no one had any business to kill Him. He was God, and He went up to heaven in the sky. But He has not only stayed there; He goes all about the world still, only we can't see Him; and He loves everybody, and He loves me, and He loves you. His name is the Lord Jesus. Have you heard of Him, dear Father? Because you never told me. My captain told me all about it: how He died because He wanted us to go to a beautiful place in the sky, and we could not have gone there if He hadn't; He didn't mind how much He was hurt as long as He could make us happy by being hurt Himself; and He likes us to speak to Him, and He always hears; and Dr. Parker says He will give me anything I ask for if it's good for me. My Good News says He likes sinners, and I have found that I am a sinner, and so is my captain. Are you a sinner, dear Father? I hope you are, because Jesus died for sinners. It is so lovely to have Jesus to talk to now. I tell Him all, and I never feel lonely no more, and He loves me—I feel He does. Nurse says you will be angry; you won't be, will you? She never tells me why. Her niece's daughter has got a husband. He is our keeper's son. Simmonds says she's a wonderful smart girl. Rex killed a little chicken yesterday; Bob beat him, and he came crying to me. Is a dog a sinner, dear Father? I hope you will write me a nice long letter, and come back soon.

Your own loving son,
Eric'"

Eric's father was smiling and looking at his son with an expression of fond delight. After a few moments he came to himself and reached out to hold his son's hand.

"Though I did not believe the doctor's report about you I could not deny that your words sounded so happy and full of life. I had to see it for myself. It is a miracle. It is too late for me, but at least I know you are finally happy."

"It's not too late, Father! Jesus loves you as much as He loves me."

"How could He love me, Eric? I have made such a mess with my life. Always running away, clinging to creeds and my mountain of books. Burn them all, Eric. Burn them all."

"O Father, just tell Jesus that you need His forgiveness; He will not turn you away. Remember the thief on the cross? Jesus said to him, 'Today you shall be with Me in paradise.' It is here in my Good News, Father.

ERIC'S GOOD NEWS.

Eric reached into his pocket and pulled out the Testament Captain Graham had given him.

"My friend, Captain Graham gave me this. It is all true. Please try to believe."

The two remained quiet for some time. Eric had run out of words and silently prayed as he held his father's hand. He could feel the strength leaving the one he loved so much. Then the silence was broken by a faint whisper. It was his father praying!

"Jesus, I am a foolish man. I have squandered my life. I have denied Your truth. Please forgive me. Please receive me into Your paradise."

Eric's father spoke no more. His breathing became weaker and weaker as the hour passed. But Eric never left his side. He sat and read from His Good News as he watched a brightness grow upon his father's face. Then his father opened his eyes and reached out as if someone called him to come, and he was gone.

"Goodbye, my Father. Tell Jesus I love Him."

Eric laid his head upon his father's hand

ERIC'S GOOD NEWS.

and wept in sorrow and joy. He felt a strong hand come to rest on his shoulder, and when he turned and saw his dear friend, he fell into his arms.

"O Captain Graham! It was wonderful. Jesus came and took his hand."

"I know my boy. I was standing in the doorway."

"I so badly wanted him to meet you."

"He will, Eric. We will meet some day. Well, my little chap," the captain said smiling, "it looks as though you have brought two wanderers into the kingdom of heaven."

"Call unto me, and I will answer thee, and show thee great and mighty things, which thou knowest not." Jeremiah 33:3

FINIS.

LAMPLIGHTER
Rare Collector's Series

The Basket of Flowers. CHRISTOPH VON SCHMID
First written in the late seventeen hundreds, this book is the first in the **Lamplighter** *Rare Collector's Series* which gave birth to Lamplighter Publishing. Come to the garden with the godly gardener, James, and his lovely daughter, Mary, and you will see why Elisabeth Elliot and Dr. Tedd Tripp so highly recommend this rare treasure.

Titus: A Comrade of The Cross. F. M. KINGSLEY
In 1894 the publisher of this book gave a $1,000 reward to any person who could write a manuscript that would set a child's heart on fire for Jesus Christ. In six weeks, the demand was so great for this book that they printed 200,000 additional copies! You and your family will fall in love with the Savior as you read this masterpiece.

A Peep Behind The Scenes. O. F. WALTON
Behind most lives, there are masks that hide our hurts and fears. As you read, or more likely cry, through this delicate work, you will understand why there is so much joy in the presence of angels when one repents. Once you read it, you will know why two-and-a-half-million copies were printed in the 1800s.

Jessica's First Prayer. H. STRETTON
What does a coffee maker have in common with a barefoot little girl? You will want to read this classic over and over again to your children as they gain new insights into compassion and mercy as never before.

Stepping Heavenward. ELIZABETH PRENTISS
Recommended by Elisabeth Elliot, Kay Arthur, and Joni Eareckson Tada, this book is for women who are seeking an intimate walk with Christ. Written in 1850, this book will reach deeply into your heart and soul with fresh spiritual insights and honest answers to questions that most women and even men would love to have settled.

Rosa of Linden Castle. CHRISTOPH VON SCHMID
In this unique Von Schmid classic, a daughter's love for her condemned father will inspire children of all ages to see that though it was meant for evil, God intends it for good.

Joel: A Boy of Galilee. ANNIE FELLOWS JOHNSTON

If you read *Titus: A Comrade of the Cross* and loved it, let me introduce you to Joel. This is a story about a handicapped boy who has to make a decision whether to follow the healer of Nazareth or the traditions of the day. You will talk about this treasure for years.

Christie's Old Organ. O.F. WALTON

This is a child's story for all ages. Join a little boy named Christie and an old organ grinder as they search for the path that leads to heaven. This dramatic story has already led children to the saving knowledge of Jesus Christ. Be prepared to cry.

Jessica's Mother. H. STRETTON AND M. HAMBY

(sequel to Jessica's First Prayer)

Rewritten by Mark Hamby, this sequel will take you through the emotions of the greatest of all sacrifices. Embittered against God and anyone who bears the name of Christ, Jessica's mother is determined to take her daughter back regardless of the consequences. This is a story of human tragedy and divine love that will inspire families to take a second look at the real meaning of the gospel of Jesus Christ.

The Lamplighter. MARIA S. CUMMINS

Written in the 1800s when lamplighters lit the street lights of the village, this story will take you on a spiritual journey depicting godly character that will inspire and attract you to live your Christian life with a higher level of integrity and excellence. Mystery, suspense, and plenty of appealing examples of integrity and honor will grip the heart of anyone who reads this masterpiece.

The Hedge of Thorns. ANONYMOUS

Based on a true story about a little boy who will do almost anything to find out what is on the other side of a hedge of thorns. Enticed and frustrated, a child is about to learn why boundaries are a necessary part of God's plan for his life.

Melody, The Story of A Child. LAURA E. RICHARDS

An inspiring and beautifully written story that invites the reader to see life through the eyes of a most unusual child. Each chapter is filled with charming freshness as a blind child weaves her gift of "seeing" into the hearts of friend and foe alike. Themes: uncompromising love, discernment, childlike honesty, faith and forgiveness.

Mary Jones and Her Bible. ANONYMOUS
Another true story of a little girl whose strongest desire in life is to possess her very own Bible. Through hard work, determination, prayer, faith, and even a twenty-five mile walk, Mary Jones does whatever it takes to obtain a copy of the Word of God. This true story will not only kindle a fire in children's hearts but give them a role model to follow that exemplifies hard work, faithfulness, and the reward of patient obedience.

The White Dove. CHRISTOPH VON SCHMID
This is another classic by the author of *The Basket of Flowers* that will once again lay a beautiful pattern of godliness for all to follow. Surrounded by knights and nobles, thieves and robbers, this story will take parent and child to the precipice of honor, nobility, sacrifice, and the meaning of true friendship. If you enjoyed *The Basket of Flowers*, you will not want to miss *The White Dove*.

Mothers of Famous Men. ARCHER WALLACE
Take a step back in time and visit with the great mothers of great men. Join Mrs. Washington, Mrs. Wesley, Mrs. Franklin, Mrs. Adams, Mrs. Lincoln, Mrs. Carnegie and many others and see what type of motherhood shaped such unusual greatness. You will enter their homes as well as their hearts, as you learn for the first time, portions of history rarely revealed. This is a book every parent and young person needs to read.

The Little Lamb. CHRISTOPH VON SCHMID
This story will teach our readers that all things do work together for good to them who love God. Parents and children will be filled with captivating suspense as they taste and see that the Lord is the God of the impossible.

Clean Your Boots, Sir? ANONYMOUS
Finally, a book for boys that I would say equals *The Basket of Flowers*! In this captivating story you will meet a brave little boy who cares for his ailing father and two baby brothers. As a shoeshine boy, the little savings that he makes each day is just enough to meet their basic needs until a small act of honesty changes his life forever. Join the shoeshine boy as he introduces your children to integrity, honesty, faith, and sacrifice, in a way that they will never forget!

The Lost Ruby. CHRISTOPH VON SCHMID

Another classic that will teach children the important lesson of honesty regardless of the cost. Also included is one of Von Schmid's finest short stories, *The Lost Child*. This is a story of mystery and intrigue as the reader learns that God allows hardships for our good.

Christie, the King's Servant. O.F. WALTON

In the sequel to *Christie's Old Organ*, we find Christie pastoring a small parish in England, where a forgotten acquaintance steps back into his life. Here in this quaint village where fishermen take to their boats for a living, there is intense drama each time the clouds and winds begin to blow. Filled with delicate love and unusual hospitality, each reader will find it hard to take when Duncan's boat is found battered and empty, days after the search has ended. Loss is never easy, but this is one loss that our readers will never forget!

True Stories of Great Americans for Young Americans.

Written for young readers, this edition of American history will inspire and reveal the character qualities and difficult circumstances that led these Americans to greatness. The seldom heard stories of George Washington, Robert E. Lee, Patrick Henry and many more will inspire and challenge young readers to value the past and guard the present as they themselves become agents of change for the future.

Stick to the Raft. MRS. GEORGE GLADSTONE

Fifteen-year-old Hans Richter travels far from home to find work in the locks of a river. His dying father teaches him that there is a Raft which will support him in the deepest waters and amid the fiercest storms. In his last moments, his father gasps, "The raft in its double meaning has been my best friend... Hold on to the Savior...". When Hans becomes the target for mischief amoung jealous peers, he must remember to "stick to the raft".

Stephen: A Soldier of the Cross. F.M. KINGSLEY

In the deserts of Egypt, a blind girl and her protective brother fall prey to desert thieves. After hearing the reports of miracles in Jerusalem, they find themselves in the midst of the greatest upheaval in history. Readers will become captivated by the intense drama that unfolds in the unrest of Jerusalem.

Probable Sons. AMY LEFEUVRE
Etched into the heart issues of unforgiveness and reconciliation, *Probable Sons* is a delightful book that will keep you smiling throughout. In a world of broken relationships, our little heroine Milly will help us tear away the layers of stubbornness and pride to provide a path that can help restore the injured from the most hurtful pain of the past. May the truths found in this little story find a resting place in many hearts that have strayed so far from home.

Boys of Grit Vol. 1, 2 & 3. ARCHER WALLACE
Children and adults will be inspired when they read about boys who overcame great misfortunes, trials, and overwhelming circumstances to become great and godly men. When so many others saw only difficulties, they saw possibilities.

The Stolen Child. CHRISTOPH VON SCHMID
Another Von Schmid classic that captures the beauty of God's creation as seen through the eyes of a child who lived in darkness most of his childhood. Lessons of responsibility and forgiveness are among the many virtues taught in this classic.

The Pillar of Fire. J.H. INGRAHAM
This is a most eloquently written book, filled with the illustrative accounts of the Prince of Tyre during his visit to Egypt over 3500 years ago. The author brings full color and inspiration to every page, while weaving his most suspenseful dramas in connection with the Scriptures. Truly, a fresh breath of literary air.

Teddy's Button. AMY LEFEUVRE
Here's a story that will warm your heart, make you laugh, and above all, will help children to understand the spiritual battle that rages in their souls. Join Teddy as he demonstrates that even a child can enlist in God's army and carry the banner of love and victory high.

The Captive. CHRISTOPH VON SCHMID
A gripping account of a sixteen-year-old boy who is captured and enslaved in a foreign country. This story will break down the barriers between cultures, and reveal the true marks of a genuine Christian.

The Wide, Wide World. SUSAN WARNER

The first book by an American author to sell one million copies, *The Wide, Wide World* is an endearing novel about a little girl who faces unrelenting affliction, only to be reminded of the One who has charge over her. On a blustery winter day, this is the book to reach for!

Shipwrecked, but not Lost. HON. MRS. DUNDAS

Impulsive, impatient young boys find themselves reaping the dreadful consequences of following foolish counsel. But there *is* a God of mercy who wants to spare his children from shipwreck!

Tom Gillies. MRS. GEORGE GLADSTONE

Tom Gillies and Dick Potter secretly meet at their favorite cave to plot the mischievous schemes which have given them so bad a name. The townspeople complain that the island is too small to hold such troublesome boys. Tom is sent away to work, where he learns that his bad habits have fastened strong chains around him, and sin has tied binding knots, making him a prisoner. He discovers the One who can untie those dreadful knots and free him to live a productive life among the people of Norton Island.

Amy and Her Brothers. ANONYMOUS

In every world-worn man there is a human heart that craves a God to trust, a Christ to lean upon—an unsatisfied heart. In *Amy and Her Brothers* the heartache and innocent faith of an orphan child paints a real-life picture of the hidden suffering all around us, challenging us to be more attentive to the hurts of those nearby.

Sir Knight of the Splendid Way. W.E. CULE

Sir Knight of the Splendid Way is a captivating allegory—a rich literary masterpiece that will encourage any weary traveler. This beautifully-bound work depicts life as a journey, reaching toward a beacon of hope in the City of the Great King. In the midst of conflict, *Sir Knight* will inspire you to press on.

Me and Nobbles. AMY LEFEUVRE

An enchanting story about imaginative Master Bobby and his beloved "friend," Nobbles. With great expectation, Bobby daily awaits his absent father's return, knowing he hasn't been forgotten. In the meantime, Bobby strives to find the secret to obtaining his very own clean white robe so that he can enter the golden gates that lead to the splendid golden city.

Tom Watkins' Mistake. EMMA LESLIE
In a day of situational ethics, this book will be an excellent opportunity to teach children that one's character is formed by one's obedience to the truth. This story is going to have a significant eternal effect upon many lives.

The Wrestler of Philippi. FANNIE NEWBERRY
Here is a story of Rome's staggering contrasts—extreme poverty amidst the wildest extravagance; treacherous dungeon life in darkness and chains amidst the splendors and amusements of luxurious court life. This dramatic unfolding of *The Wrestler of Philippi* will grip your heart as you experience the true test of loyalty and the triumph of faith!

The Bird's Nest. CHRISTOPH VON SCHMID
Strength of character lies in the determination to hold on to truth regardless of circumstances or consequences. The hero in this story proves to us that every seemingly insignificant deed is noticed by God.

Buried in the Snow. FRANZ HOFFMAN
You will be blessed by the gentle wisdom of an old grandfather and the unconditional love of his grandson as they come face to face with one of the most difficult decisions of their lives. From the depths of despair to the pinnacle of blessing, this dramatic encounter will surely elicit a full spectrum of emotional responses.

The White Knights. W.E. CULE
It all started that lonely night in the chapel. Those few dreadful moments when he not only *heard* the silence, he could *feel* it. That night Horace passed the test—his life as a knight had begun. The motto of The White Knights, following that of King Arthur, *"To ride abroad redressing human wrongs,"* was a high order to fill. Little did they know what different shapes that would take, and what adventures and challenges lie ahead. But none of that mattered, for they all agreed, *"The spirit's the thing!"*

A Puzzling Pair. AMY LEFEUVRE
Inseparable twins, Guy and Berry are bursting with creativity and spunk. They are on a mission…to fill Guy's very big picture of the second coming of Jesus with all the people who are ready to meet Him! But his picture must be true, and time is running out! This rather unique approach to evangelism is as pure, bold, and simple as it gets!

Little Sir Galahad. LILLIAN HOLMES

Since the "sad thing" happened, young David spends his days sitting beside the window, watching the children and working people of Alverton pass by. But he is so rich in sunny smiles and imaginative play that they have no reason to call him "Poor David." Young David's greatest desire is to become strong again, but he learns that real strength comes in fighting his own temper and choosing to do what is right, especially when it is so difficult! Because of his pure heart, inner strength, and noble deeds, he is donned "Sir Galahad," an honorable title for one "whose strength is as the strength of ten because his heart is pure."

The Cross Triumphant. FLORENCE KINGSLEY

This extraordinary sequel to Titus and Stephen will take the reader on an unforgettable journey seventeen years after the crucifixion. Rich in biblical history, Mrs. Kingsley is able to weave several dramatic themes that climax at the devastating destruction of Jerusalem. Eleven hundred thousand persons are said to have perished during the siege, while nearly a hundred thousand were made prisoners. It was in the midst of this deep tribulation that Mrs. Kingsley births hope during one of the most tragic events in history. If you enjoyed Titus, you will not want to miss this classic!

Winter's Folly . O.F. WALTON

Winter's Folly is a tender story of lonely Old Man Winter, who demonstrates the epitome of selfless love. In the meantime, young Myrtle is determined to bring comfort and cheer to this misunderstood, desolate old man. This true-to-life story reminds us once again that when life seems to hold more than we can bear, we can rest assured that we have a loving God who is orchestrating events for our good.

The Stranger At Home VARIOUS AUTHORS

The Stranger at Home, along with its accompanying stories, *The Coveted Bonnet* and *The Cords of Sin* might seem a little "hard-edged," but it is, without a doubt, provocative. The folly of permissive parenting, and the inevitable consequences of obstinacy, disobedience, lying, and vanity are brought forth with "not-so-subtle" clarity.

Fireside Readings Vol. 2. VARIOUS AUTHORS
In our day of situation ethics and relativism, it is refreshing to read a story like *Annie, the Flower Girl* who, in spite of the fact that she'd be helping her poor grandmother, decides to do the right thing, simply because it is right to do right! In this second volume, the consequences of covetousness, jealousy, and disobedience ring loud and clear, while the rewards of honesty, obedience and contentment bring forth a sense of inner satisfaction.

The Boy Who Never Lost A Chance. ANNETTE LYSTER
Roger Read has learned from his grandfather never to miss a "chance." His hard work, honesty, and diligence are richly rewarded. But having become self-absorbed in his own pursuits, Roger finally realizes something is missing in his life, and he can't seem to find it—until his true friend Jack Sparling helps him to see the best "chance" of all! If you want to inspire your children with an entrepreneurial spirit, balanced with service for God, this is a must-read!

The House of Love. ELIZABETH CHENEY
Aurelia Wilde is cruelly selfish and downright miserable—a victim of her mother's desperate attempts to place her delicate, "prized possession" on an unreachable pedestal. But her glory is only surface deep. Aurelia's ungrateful, complaining spirit is a stark contrast to that of her servant-girl, Doris. She knows that God is Love, and the "house of the Lord" must be the House of Love. Her many talents and her cheerful disposition cause her to be loved and appreciated, even by the notable residents of Waverly Manor. How jealousy swells within Aurelia's vengeful mother! She'll get even yet…

Tales of the Kingdom. MAINS
Back in print by popular demand, this allegorical children's classic will take you on a journey to the enchanted city as you relive the wonderful experiences of God's great deliverance. I would place this treasure on an equal with *Chronicles of Narnia and Pilgrim's Progress.*

The Three Weavers. ANNIE FELLOWS JOHNSTON
Fathers and daughters will take a journey back to Camelot and learn the unforgettable lessons of virtue and vice.

The Hidden Hand E.D.E.N. SOUTHWORTH
Reader BEWARE—this is NOT your typical Rare Collector book! Strewn with mystery and suspense that never lets up, *The Hidden Hand* will keep you on the edge of your seat! There are not too many books that cause me to laugh aloud (even when I'm alone!) Truly laughter is like medicine, giving health to the bones! But please don't let the feisty, mischievous character of 17-year-old Capitola and the cantankerous personality of Old Hurricane derail you from seeing the gracious providence of an all-wise God. (For ages 16 and up.)

To order a catalog, call us toll free at 1-888-246-7735, email us at mail@lamplighterpublishing.com, or visit our website at www.lamplighterpublishing.com.

MAKING READY A PEOPLE PREPARED FOR THE LORD